ANCIENT PHOENICIA

D1476413

015

C333023772

Classical World Series

Classical World Series

ANCIENT PHOENICIA

An Introduction

Mark Woolmer

Bristol Classical Press

First published in 2011 by
Bristol Classical Press
an imprint of
Bloomsbury Academic
Bloomsbury Publishing Plc
36 Soho Square,
London W1D 3QY

CIP records for this book are available from the
British Library and the Library of Congress

ISBN 978-1-85399-734-1

Typeset by Ray Davies
Printed and bound in Great Britain by
CPI Antony Rowe, Chippenham and Eastbourne

www.bloomsburyacademic.com

Contents

Acknowledgements

I am extremely grateful to Roger Rees for inviting me to write this book; to Justine Wolfenden and Clemence Schultze for taking the time and effort to read it and improve its structure and expression; to Jennifer Ingleheart and Sian Lewis for making very many helpful suggestions on substance and presentation; to my mother and father Dina and Nigel Woolmer, and my good friend Susie Walton for the love and support during what was at times a difficult process; to Lloyd Llewellyn-Jones and Stephanie Winder for the chance to travel the Middle East; to the students of Edinburgh and St Andrews Universities for providing constructive feedback and suggestions while taking my courses; and to the various institutions and individuals who kindly granted me permission to reproduce their photos. None should be supposed to agree with my arguments, let alone share responsibility for any errors.

This book is dedicated in loving memory of Alexandra Smith, a true friend whose boundless energy and enthusiasm will be forever missed.

Introduction

The Phoenicians were a clever race, who prospered in war and peace. They excelled in writing and literature, and in other arts, in seamanship, in naval warfare, and in ruling an empire. (Pomponius Mela 1.12)

The people known to us as the Phoenicians were an enigmatic and often misunderstood and maligned group in antiquity. On the one hand they were praised as learned scribes who disseminated the alphabet, lauded as exceptional seafarers and navigators who explored previously unknown regions and who helped define the boundaries of the ancient world, renowned as skilful artists and accomplished engineers who produced exceptional works of art, and finally deemed to be traders par excellence who could be relied upon to acquire any natural resource or commodity. However, in contrast to these positive depictions, the Phoenicians were also derided as hucksters and cheats, men who could not be trusted and who were more interested in money than morality; they were maligned as pirates and thieves; and seen as impious men ready to prostitute their daughters or sacrifice their children in order to appease their blood-thirsty deities. This contradiction of views is reflected in modern scholarship. This is perhaps unsurprising as, until the middle of the twentieth century, there had been no systematic excavation even of such important Phoenician sites as Tyre, Byblos and Sidon. Scholars writing before the mid-twentieth century were solely reliant on the literary evidence, a situation made worse by the fragmentary survival of the Phoenicians' own written histories and mythologies. In an ironic twist of fate, the very civilisation responsible for disseminating the alphabet to the west left virtually no written legacy. Early scholars therefore sought to fill the gaps in their knowledge by using Assyrian, Babylonian, Israelite, Greek and Roman records, most of which present a negative view of the Phoenicians. The result was a heavily distorted picture of Phoenician culture, religion and society.

The hostile view presented by contemporary writers outside Phoenicia is perhaps understandable. The Assyrian accounts, which mainly occur in royal inscriptions and letters, generally recount the conquest of a number of the Phoenician city-states and thereby present the Phoenicians in terms of a conquered foe. The Bible, the most comprehensive literary source for Phoenician history, provides indirect evidence for Phoenician culture and religion but its use is limited by the hostile view it takes of non-Israelite beliefs and customs. The usefulness of books such as Kings and Chronicles, which provide detailed accounts of the relationship between Israelite rulers and their Phoenician counterparts, is counterbalanced by the prophecies of Isaiah and Ezekiel who predicted the spectacular demise of the decadent Phoenician cities of Sidon and Tyre. The Greeks had a negative view of the Phoenicians, regarding Phoenician traders as responsible for promoting greed and luxury among their citizenry, a situation which led to the undermining of traditional values and a restructuring of established hierarchies. Similarly, the Romans, who fought a series of long wars against the Phoenician colonists of Carthage, frequently display the bitterness associated with the accounts of authors writing about a particularly hated adversary. Despite later Greek and Roman authors such as Eusebius of Caesarea and Philo of Byblos attempting to offer a more sympathetic view of Phoenicia, ultimately their accounts were as distorted as those of their predecessors.

Although all these sources shed some light on the military and commercial affairs of the Phoenician cities, they record little detail about the political, religious, economic and cultural development of Phoenicia. We must therefore turn to archaeology and the evidence it can offer in order to reconstruct Phoenician society and culture. This evidence bears witness to the close relationship that Phoenicia enjoyed with its Mediterranean neighbours. For instance, the Phoenicians' eclectic artistic style is a testament to their wide-reaching trade networks and preoccupation with developing artefacts for export to foreign markets. The material evidence can also help to illuminate aspects of Phoenician culture left unrecorded in the literary texts. However, a problem facing the student or general reader is the lack of accessible, up-to-date literature examining Phoenician archaeology. Such literature as exists is either scattered in a multitude of journal articles, written in foreign languages, or in books that are out of print, or in conference proceedings not easily accessible to the non-specialist reader. Consequently, this book provides a schematic overview of Phoenicia and Phoenician history in conjunction with an examination of the present state of archaeological investigation. It examines approximately a thousand years of Phoenician history from the late Bronze Age to the start of the Hellenistic period (i.e. from c. 1300 to 300 BC). With such a wide focus it is impossible to explain all the complexities of

Phoenician civilisation; rather the aim is to illuminate themes and topics which can provide a solid foundation for more in-depth study. This volume therefore combines a general introduction to the identity, culture and history of the Phoenicians with a number of case studies designed to highlight topics of particular interest or importance. Finally, illustrations in a book of this size must inevitably be restricted and thus each image has been chosen because it illuminates a particular topic or idea. This is in no way an exhaustive collection and these images may easily be supplemented by the books, guides and websites that have been included in the suggested further reading at the back of the book.

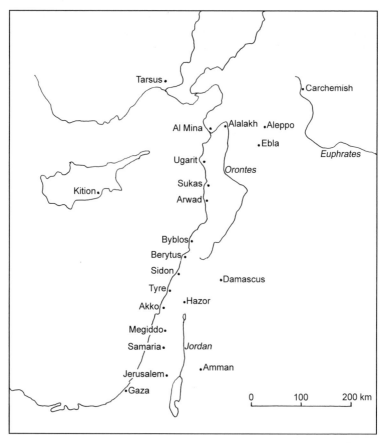

Fig. 1. Map of the Phoenician coastline.

Chapter 1

Defining the Phoenicians: Land, Language, Name and People

There is no clear-cut definition of the Phoenicians as a people with a recognisable territory of their own, a homogeneous language and a shared historical and cultural heritage. As an ethnic group the Phoenicians were the descendants of the Canaanites, a race of people who lived in a tract of land roughly covering modern day Lebanon and Israel. However, the Canaanites were never a genuinely cohesive ethnic group; a variety of cultures and peoples were denoted by the term. For example, the biblical writers speak of the 'Canaanites' as being just one of a multiplicity of ethnic groups residing in the region known as 'Canaan'. Other tribes and cultures included the Amorites, Hivites, Girgashites, Jebusites and Perizzites. Consequently 'Canaanite' was used in a non-specific manner and could refer to an individual (or group) from any one of these tribes. To complicate matters further, the region designated as 'Canaan' was also defined imprecisely. Over time the groups of Canaanites dwelling along the coastline of modern Lebanon were seen to be different from the tribes further inland, and thus these coastal inhabitants became known as Phoenicians. In modern scholarship it is customary to use the term 'Canaanite' to demarcate those people who spoke North West Semitic and lived in the territory of Syria-Palestine from the beginning of the second millennium BC until *c.* 1200 BC. From 1200 BC until the conquests of Alexander the Great in 333 BC it is customary to identify the 'Canaanite' inhabitants of the regions of modern day Lebanon and coastal Syria as 'Phoenicians'. The year 1200 was fixed by scholars as it marked the end of the political turbulence and upheavals which had accompanied the transition from the Bronze to the Iron Age. After 1200 the city-states of coastal Canaan began to develop their own unique cultural identity and it is at this moment they became the distinct ethnic group known to history as the Phoenicians.

What's in a name?
The name by which history has remembered the Phoenicians (*phoínix*) is of Greek origin and was used by the Greeks to identify an eastern people

who shared a number of cultural characteristics and traits. The term was first used some time between the ninth and seventh centuries BC, but, significantly, it has no known equivalent in any of the languages of the ancient Near East. The linguistic root of *phoínix* is therefore neither Phoenician nor Semitic and presents an as yet unsolved etymological conundrum. Even the Greeks were unclear on the origins of the word, and Greek authors often try to offer an explanation for it. The term *phoínix* was also used to denote a reddish-purple colour, leading some scholars to suggest that its use to designate an ethnic group was a deliberate allusion to the purple textile industry for which the Phoenicians were to become famed. According to this tradition, the term 'Phoenician' was derived from the Greek word *phoinós* which can be translated as either 'red', 'blood', 'to stain with blood' or 'death'. If this is accepted, then the name Phoenicia should be understood as either 'the country of purple dyers' or 'the land of purple cloth'. Another popular theory is found in Pliny, who postulates that there is a connection between the name 'Phoenician' and the eponymous hero *Phoínix*. Pliny recounts a legend in which the discovery of purple dye is a chance event attributed to a shepherd and his dog. The shepherd's dog bites into a mollusc – presumably the murex – and stains itself red. The dog is then brought before the king of Tyre, Phoinix, who adopts the colour as an emblem of royalty. Although Pliny's is the only surviving written account of the legend, a number of coins from Tyre are believed to depict the shepherd's dog, suggesting that the myth had Phoenician origins.

The issue of ethnicity raises an even more contentious question: did the Phoenicians, in fact, have a 'national' identity? The city-states of Tyre, Byblos, Sidon and Arwad were all fiercely independent and rarely cooperated with each other unless faced with a common threat. Adding to the confusion is the fact that the Phoenicians were frequently referred to by foreign authors simply by the name of their city of origin, for instance, Tyrians, Giblites, Sidonians, etc. Roman authors do little to ease the confusion as they simply use the term *phoenix*, a transcription into Latin of the Greek *phoínix*. Scholars agree that the Phoenicians never referred to themselves as 'Phoenician', but with the lack of any alternative historians have adopted the title bestowed on them by the Greeks. When discussing the 'Phoenicians' it is also worth remembering that the cities of Phoenicia were a meeting-ground for people of different ethnic backgrounds and cultures. The inhabitants of cities such as Tyre, Sidon and Byblos would have been an amalgam of different tribes, races and languages, similar perhaps to the ethnic diversity of fifth- and fourth-century Athens, or modern Beirut. The number of languages and regional dialects found on inscriptions from this region attests to this ethnic blending. Consequently, the Phoenicians were not a closed society and the major civic centres would have had a cosmopolitan feel to them.

The climate and topography of Phoenicia

According to classical authors, the Phoenicians occupied the entire Levantine coast, but archaeology has shown that the heartland of Phoenicia was considerably smaller. After the turmoil that marked the end of the Bronze Age, the land controlled by the Phoenician city-states had been reduced from a distance of 500 km from north to south, to a distance of a little over 200 km. The territory which modern scholars have designated as *Phoiníke* extends along the coastline of the Eastern Mediterranean, its boundaries roughly corresponding to those of modern Lebanon. The region was therefore situated between the mountains of Lebanon to the east and the Mediterranean to the west and was, in essence, a long narrow strip of land. The distance between the coast and the mountains was on average a mere 30 km. The mountains bordering Phoenicia not only protected the region from incursions from the east but also provided fresh water, as a number of mountain rivers crisscrossed the region on their way seawards. The unique geography of Phoenicia resulted in a patchwork of independent city-states separated by river valleys and mountain spurs. This landscape encouraged political individualism and isolation and prevented the formation of a unified state, even during periods of intense pressure from empires such as Egypt or Assyria. The Phoenician city-states can therefore be considered as equally independent and culturally diverse as the *poleis* of classical Greece.

In general, the Phoenician climate was mild, not unlike that of modern Lebanon: the soil was rich in minerals and nutrients washed down from the mountains by the frequent, often torrential, rainstorms. Importantly, during the winter months there was also high rainfall across the plains: this penetrated deep into the loamy soil, helping to fertilise it. Spring began in March and brought with it the end of the rainy season; between May and September there was virtually no rainfall. In October the weather once again became cooler, the rains resumed, and the annual cycle began afresh. Due to its topography and climate Phoenicia was one of the most fertile countries in the Levant. However, despite the fertility of the low lying agricultural land, the area was not extensive. As the population increased, demand quickly outgrew the productive capacity of the land, and the Phoenicians were never self-sufficient in terms of foodstuffs. Despite the limited area of arable land, agriculture was well-developed: wheat, vines, fruit trees, and olives are known to have been grown in significant quantities (see Chapter 5 for more details). In addition to their agricultural output, the Phoenician cities also had access to plentiful game. The mountainous regions to the east of Phoenicia teemed with panthers, bears, hyenas, wolves, jackals and hares, all of which were excellent sources of meat. Phoenicia's greatest natural resource, however, was the extensive forests that covered much of the region. These provided abundant supplies of cypresses, pines and above all cedars which were famed throughout the ancient Near East. Cedars were particularly prized because they were ideally suited for the construction of buildings and ships and could therefore be traded with a number of states, including Egypt, Israel, Assyria and Babylon. The mountains of Phoenicia also provided an array of mineral resources. Archaeological excavations have shown that the Phoenicians undertook extensive mining of the mountains in order to acquire marble, lignite, iron and a fine grained sand which they used in the manufacture of glass. Moreover, the principal cities of Phoenicia were all situated either on the coast, on mainland promontories that dominated a bay, or in small natural inlets. By situating their cities in coastal locations the Phoenicians gained access to a variety of marine resources including fish, molluscs and most importantly salt. On the whole, the landscape of Phoenicia provided the inhabitants with excellent resources. However, these resources were not plentiful enough to enable self-sufficiency: thus necessity forced the Phoenicians to pursue an active trade policy.

Language
The Phoenician tongue belongs to a family of languages known as North West Semitic, which is traditionally divided into two groups, Canaanite and Aramaic. The Phoenician language is a member of the Canaanite group, to which Hebrew, Ammonite, Moabite and Edomite belong. At its height the Phoenician dialect was widespread throughout the Levant and its prevalence in monumental royal inscriptions underscores its importance as a language of diplomacy. Its use by a variety of ethnic groups resulted in the language evolving rapidly and gave rise to a number of innovations and grammatical developments. Furthermore, due to the longevity of the language and the division of Phoenicia into various kingdoms, a number of unique regional dialects emerged: examples of these have been identified at Byblos, Cyprus, Northern Syria and Southern Anatolia. The Byblian vernacular, for instance, has a tendency to be archaising when compared to the others. Moreover, the Byblian, Cypriot and Sidonian scripts also exhibit regional differences in their letter formation. The dominant linguistic form was unsurprisingly the dialect that was shared by Tyre and Sidon, and this has become known as 'standard

Phoenician'. The legacy of the Phoenician language has been undermined by the almost complete loss of the literary corpus. Although the classical authors record that there were a number of great Phoenician texts which explored a diverse array of subjects including history, philosophy, law, religion, natural history and economics, not a single fragment has survived in its original form.

The alphabet and its dissemination

There is a general consensus that the modern linear alphabet originated somewhere in the Levant during the second millennium BC. In antiquity it was a commonly held belief that Phoenicians invented the alphabet, but this has proved incorrect. There is still much debate concerning the precise date and point of origin for the alphabet and it remains unclear which ethnic group first invented it or how it was transmitted to the Phoenicians. However, what can safely be concluded is that the alphabetic principle was certainly invented earlier than the Phoenician period but that the development of convenient signs with which to represent letters and sounds was a Phoenician innovation (see Fig. 2). The Phoenician alphabet contains 20 consonants and is well documented on early Byblian monuments such as the sarcophagus of Ahiram and the statues of Sheshonq I and Osorkon (two Egyptian pharaohs). Even at this early stage the stance and form of the various letters seem to have been fixed. Moreover, the direction in which the script was written and read was already established as being horizontal and in a uniformly sinistrograde fashion (i.e. from right to left). In these early inscriptions individual words were separated by short vertical strokes but in later Phoenician texts the words were presented in an unbroken sequence, with many straddling two lines of text if

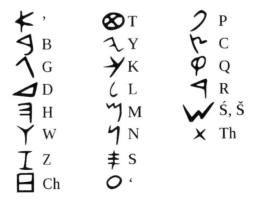

Fig. 2. The Phoenician alphabet.

they could not be fitted onto one. There is no evidence to suggest the Phoenician alphabet was ever vocalised.

The epigraphic evidence shows that the Phoenician alphabet was quickly transmitted beyond the borders of Phoenicia. By the ninth century a number of neighbouring languages had adopted the system and adapted it to their own needs; these included Ammonite, Aramaic, Edomite, Hebrew and Moabite. As the Phoenicians undertook commercial ventures throughout the Mediterranean they exported their language and alphabet alongside their commodities. In c. 900 BC Crete and Cyprus were the first non-Levantine cultures to adopt the Phoenician alphabet. Just over a century later the Phoenician alphabetic tradition can be found emerging in the western Mediterranean in places such as southern Spain and Sardinia. Interestingly, the Phoenician language, replaced by Aramaic and Greek, died out earlier in Phoenicia itself than in the western colonies.

Of those cultures which adopted the Phoenician alphabet, the Greeks were the most proactive in embracing and developing it. Herodotus states: 'The Phoenicians who came to Cadmus ... among other types of learning, brought into Hellas the alphabet, which had hitherto been unknown, as I think, to the Greeks.' The names, shapes, values, and order of the various Greek letters clearly attest a Phoenician influence. In terms of the date at which the Greeks adopted the Phoenician alphabet there is still a huge diversity of opinion, estimates range from the mid-second millennium to the eighth century BC. Traditionally a date of c. 850 BC has been proposed because of the similarities between the letter forms of early Greek and ninth-century Phoenician. However, recent archaeological research has compared Greek graffiti found on pottery shards – the earliest of which date to the second quarter of the eighth century – with mainland Phoenician inscriptions and concluded that a transmission date of c. 950 BC is more likely. Theories on the place of transmission also vary wildly with a multiplicity of locations suggested: these include the Greek mainland, Crete, Euboea, Rhodes, western Asia Minor, the Levant and Cyprus. Although Euboea has become the site generally favoured by scholars, mainly due to its close commercial links with Phoenicia, the other suggestions are equally plausible.

Chapter 2

A General History of Phoenicia

Thanks to ongoing archaeological excavations under the auspices of the British Museum, the National Museum of Beirut, and the American University of Beirut, our knowledge of Phoenician history has improved significantly in recent years. The systematic excavation of a number of important Phoenician sites has provided a wealth of evidence, both material and epigraphic, which has helped to illuminate the history of Phoenicia. For example, thanks to evidence provided by archaeology, the growing power of the Byblian monarchs during the Early Bronze Age is now well-attested in both the epigraphic and material records. Despite this, however, our knowledge of Phoenician history is still very irregular and conditioned by the available documentation. Consequently, any reconstruction of Phoenician history is almost entirely founded on indirect sources.

One direct source, the so-called 'annals of Tyre', is unfortunately transmitted only indirectly and in fragmentary form by the ancient authors Josephus and Menander of Ephesus. The passages quoted by these authors refer to two periods of Phoenician history and provide details about various kings and important political events. The indirect transmission of this information obviously adds to the risk of its misinterpretation, but when comparisons are made with other literary sources and the archaeological evidence, it has been shown to be remarkably accurate. Aside from the works of Josephus and Menander, the Phoenician cities are also mentioned in a number of Egyptian and Mesopotamian sources such as the Assyrian and Hittite annals, the Egyptian text *The Tale of Wen-Amon*, and the Amarna Letters (see Fig. 4). Although many of these texts record military expeditions against the cities of Canaan and Phoenicia, they are useful for constructing an overview of Phoenician history.

Another important source is the Old Testament, whose historical books provide detailed accounts of the relationship between Phoenician cities and the fledgling state of Israel. Despite the fragmentary nature of the data it contains, the Old Testament still offers a more sustained narrative than any other source. For instance, the biblical books 1 and 2 Kings contain a detailed record of the relationship between Solomon and Hiram, king of

Fig. 3. Chronology of Phoenician history.

Era	Dates (BC)	Primary characteristics
Palaeolithic	before *c.* 18000	Hunter-gatherer society. First use of stone tools.
Mesolithic	*c.* 18000-8000	Transitional period towards farmer-herder societies. The first domestication of animals.
Neolithic	*c.* 8000-4500	Formalisation of farmer-herder societies. First known town, Jericho, is built in the Levant.
Chalcolithic	*c.* 4500-3500	The development of metal working and the first use of metal tools. Initial trading contact between Egypt and Byblos is established.
Early Bronze Age (EB)	3500-2000	The Canaanites begin to settle the Syrian coast; Tyre and Sidon are founded. Innovations such as the wheel and writing introduced.
Middle Bronze Age (MB)	2000-1550	Canaan under Egyptian rule after the campaigns of Tuthmosis I and his grandson Tuthmosis III.
Late Bronze Age (LB)	1550-1200	Phoenicians formalise the alphabet and discover Tyrian purple. Economic, political and military crises lead to the destruction/abandonment of a number of key Phoenician cities.

Period	Date	Description
Iron Age I (IA I)	1200-900	The Sea Peoples and Philistines introduce iron technology into Asia. The Phoenician seaports become major commercial powers. The first Phoenician colonies are founded on the Atlantic coast.
Iron Age II (IA II)	900-586	The Assyrian empire rises to prominence and subjugates Canaan and the Phoenician city-states. Main period of Phoenician colonisation.
Babylonian Period	586-539	Phoenicia and the Levant annexed into the Babylonian empire. Nebuchadnezzar undertakes a thirteen-year siege of Tyre.
Persian Period	539-332	Cyrus the Great conquers Canaan and Palestine, bringing the Phoenician cities under Persian rule. The Phoenician cities pay tribute to Persia and provide vessels for the Great King's navy.
Alexander the Great	336-323	Alexander the Great conquers the Persian empire; the Phoenician states lose their independence.
Hellenistic Period	332-63	Phoenicia becomes part of the Ptolemaic empire. After the battle at Panion (200 BC), the Seleucids seize control of Phoenicia and it remains under Seleucid rule until the Roman conquest of Syria.
Roman Period	63 BC - 324 AD	Tyre becomes a Roman colony. Phoenicia's *entrepôts* are replaced by new Roman *emporia* and civic centres.

Tyre. Such information is particularly important because it was recorded by scribes working in a society that had close economic and political links with Phoenicia. A significant contribution to our understanding of Phoenician history is also made by Greek and Roman historians such as Herodotus, Thucydides, Xenophon, Diodorus Siculus, Arrian, Eusebius of Caesarea and Philo of Byblos, to whom we owe much of our information about the period immediately preceding the campaigns of Alexander the Great. By combining these diverse sources it becomes possible to offer a plausible reconstruction of Phoenician history.

Before 1200 BC
From the beginning of the third millennium BC the peoples of Syria-Palestine were gravitating towards the development of large cities such as Byblos, Tyre and Megiddo. These cities rose to greater prominence as they came to foster close political and commercial relationships with Mesopotamia and Egypt. Recent archaeological excavations at Ebla (an ancient city in northern Syria) have revealed that between *c.* 2500-2300 BC the Canaanite cities of *A-ra-wa-ad* (Arwad), *Sa-ra-pa-at* (Sarepta), *Ak-zi-u* (Akhziv), *Gub-lu* (Byblos), *Ba-u-ra-at-u* (Beirut), *Za-a-ru* (Tyre), and *Si-du-na-a* (Sidon) became intermediaries in the trade between the

Fig. 4. Clay tablet containing a letter, written in cuneiform, from king Ammunira of Beirut to the pharaoh of Egypt (courtesy of the British Museum).

Syrian states and Egypt, in particular the regions of the Nile valley. In early accounts Byblos is recorded as the chief commercial centre in Canaan, often being described as the 'capital' of the region. In order to acquire metals, fabrics, wines, oils, and livestock from Ebla, the Canaanite cities exported linen and worked metals eastwards into the heartland of Asia Minor. By the late Bronze Age it is therefore possible to identify two of the characteristic features that would later come to define the Phoenician world: a willingness to become intermediaries between the Asiatic interior of the Near East and the various cities and states bordering the Mediterranean, and the importance of trade and commerce to Phoenicia's social, economic and political infrastructures. Tyre also appears repeatedly in the diplomatic documents dating to this period. Although not rivalling the power and prestige of its northern neighbour, Tyre was nevertheless prosperous during this period, a fact attested by the monumental building programmes that archaeologists have begun to uncover. However, by the end of the Early Bronze Age both Byblos and Tyre show signs that they had been abandoned or destroyed. The period c. 2300 – c. 1900 BC also sees the invasion of Syria-Palestine by the nomadic tribes of Amurru, resulting in a sharp decline in the volume of seaborne commerce between the Canaanite cities and Egypt. These nomads attacked and destroyed many of the principal Canaanite towns and villages before finally colonising the regions surrounding Aleppo and Mari. Once the crisis had abated both Byblos and Tyre quickly began to recover and then prosper. For much of the Canaanite middle Bronze Age, Egypt again held sway over the foremost cities of Canaan, with Byblos being considered the bridgehead of Egypt's dominance over the Levant. However, contemporary Egyptian texts also indicate that there was an independent monarchy at Tyre, and during the late Bonze Age it was Byblos, Ugarit and Tyre that took a central role in creating trade networks that linked Egypt, Syria-Palestine and Mesopotamia with the rest of the Mediterranean.

The Canaanite Bronze Age was brought to an abrupt end by a series of economic and socio-political crises. The complete destruction and abandonment of Ugarit combined with the Israelite invasion of the region in c. 1230 BC caused widespread disruption. This was compounded by the conquest of the Levant by the so-called 'Sea Peoples' (a loose confederacy of seafaring raiders that attacked the Levantine coast during the late Bronze Age). One group of these 'Sea Peoples', the Philistines, having laid waste to the Hittite empire and destroyed a number of Canaanite cities, occupied the southern coastal region of Canaan, causing further upheaval. In addition to disruption caused by human factors, geological surveys have shown that environmental and climatic changes caused a gradual rise in both temperature and sea level. This had a negative impact on agriculture and caused short-term food shortages. Although the invasion of the 'Sea Peoples' has traditionally been considered the primary destabilising factor during the late Bronze Age, in all probability it was the combination of these traumatic events which caused such extreme political upheavals. This sustained period of crisis resulted in a social, economic and political reordering of Canaan and, ultimately, the designation of 'Phoenicia' as an independent region. The study of this phase of Phoenician history poses numerous problems as the decline in economic and political activity led to a parallel decline in documentation.

The twelfth century BC

After the 'crisis' of the late thirteenth century there are indications that, despite the destruction wrought upon many of the Bronze Age centres such as Ugarit, a few of the Phoenician cities managed a rapid recovery. In particular both Byblos and Sidon show signs of economic growth and expansion which enabled them to dominate the Phoenician political scene during the Early Iron Age (c. 1150-900 BC). In general, the events of the early years of the Phoenician Iron Age are difficult to recover due to the paucity of both literary and archaeological evidence. The earliest surviving textual source is an inscription of the Assyrian king Tiglath-Pileser I (1114-1076 BC), who undertook a campaign against the Phoenicians in order to gain access to their supplies of cedar wood. During the course of this campaign Tiglath-Pileser records that he subjugated and then received tribute from the 'chief' Phoenician cities of Byblos, Sidon and Arwad. Tyre is absent from this list, suggesting that the Assyrian king saw the city as politically insignificant. The most important document illuminating this period is the account of Wen-Amon, a senior Egyptian official in the Theban temple of Amon-Ra, who was sent by the High Priest Herihor as an envoy to Phoenicia, charged with the task of acquiring cedar wood for the construction of a new sacred barge for Amon. The account of his journey provides a detailed description of the Phoenician coast during the period 1075-1060 BC. Wen-Amon describes Byblos as the most powerful and influential harbour town, closely followed by Sidon: Tyre is ascribed a much lower status.

As a consequence of their pre-eminence, Byblos and Sidon were in a privileged position when it came to international diplomacy, a fact attested by the treatment of Wen-Amon at the hands of his Phoenician hosts. Rather than merely acquiescing to the Egyptian demands, the Byblian prince, Zakarbal, insisted that payment be sent from Egypt before any timber was dispatched. This somewhat indifferent treatment reflects a changing political reality: whereas previously Byblos had been subservient to Egypt, this was no longer true. Egypt's political and economic power was in slow decline: thus Zakarbal was confident enough to stand his ground and insist on payment upfront. The account of Wen-Amon not only highlights the profitability of the cedar trade but also provides an important insight into the wealth and resources at the disposal of the Byblian royal house. However, shortly after Wen-Amon's visit the economic and political strength of Byblos was to be undermined by Tyre. During the eleventh and tenth centuries Tyre's rise to become an undisputed commercial powerhouse caused considerable disruption to established trade networks, in particular those controlled by Byblos. By implementing a series of aggressive commercial measures Tyre was able to increase its own economic and political influence at the expense of its neighbours. Ultimately Byblos was hit hardest by Tyre's success, so we know little more than the names of some of Zakarbal's successors: even the renowned Byblian king Ahiram remains shrouded in mystery.

The eleventh century BC
Archaeological research has revealed that during the early eleventh century there were close cultural connections between Phoenicia, Palestine and Cyprus. Common elements in the material culture of these regions suggest that contact was both extensive and sustained. This interaction stimulated the development of far-reaching trade networks, a number of which have been traced thanks to the efforts of various archaeologists who have diligently analysed pottery distribution around the Mediterranean. The archaeological record reveals that by the latter half of the eleventh century the cities of Phoenicia were undertaking a period of commercial expansion, both at home and overseas. This would facilitate the colonisation drive that became a defining aspect of Phoenician history in the tenth century.

The latter half of the eleventh century also gave rise to two important technological innovations: the creation of bichrome (two-colour) pottery and the development of urbanism. The distribution of bichrome pottery provides unrivalled evidence for the Phoenicians' wide-ranging commercial interests throughout Anatolia, Egypt and the Levant. This type of pottery has now been discovered all along the Levantine coast, from Tell Sukas in the north to the Mount Carmel peninsula in the south, and in Syria (the Amuq plain and Homos region), northern Palestine (including sites such as Galilee, Megiddo, and Beth Shemesh), Philistia (Tell Qasile, Tell Masos), and the Nile Delta (Tell er-Retabeh). The second innovation, urbanism, was to have a profound impact on the Phoenician city-states.

At Tyre the first signs of urbanism can be identified early in eleventh century and are manifest in the rebuilding of the city's destroyed walls and buildings. The architectural plans of both Tyre and Sarepta reveal significant changes to their layout, with the newly reconstructed cities beginning to utilise terracing and new methods of construction. For instance, the city walls at Sarepta were now reconstructed using the 'pier-and-rubble' technique; a typical feature of Phoenician architecture during the late Iron Age. Walls constructed using the 'pier-and-rubble' technique were primarily built from fieldstones (i.e. unshaped stones) with large, well-hewn blocks being deployed to strengthen strategically weak points, like entrances and intersections (Phoenician architecture and construction techniques will be addressed in more detail in Chapter 4). The archaeological record also indicates that simultaneous to their economic expansion, Phoenician city-states also undertook a series of military incursions into Galilee and the regions located along the coast of Northern Israel.

During this period of military and economic expansion one Phoenician city was to come to the fore: Sidon. Both the literary and archaeological records attest to the pre-eminence of Sidon, with the biblical books of Joshua, Judges and Samuel recording that the city held sway over a wide territory. In fact the term 'Sidonian' was often used by the biblical authors as a generic term to indicate someone of Canaanite or Phoenician origin. Similarly the Amarna Letters suggest that it was Sidon and then Arwad that possessed the largest number of naval vessels, chariot corps and infantry units, not Tyre or Byblos as had previously been the case. Sidon's strength in this period was a consequence of its access to fertile agricultural land. In addition to its own agriculturally rich coastal plains, it also controlled the fertile land located to the east of the city. Moreover, this territory also provided access to the lucrative overland trade routes that ran southwards from Syria to upper Jordon. Tyre, in contrast, as an island city was totally dependent on continued access to its mainland resources, could be easily contained by its enemies. This situation is most clearly illustrated in a series of letters found in the Amarna archive, which record that a contingent of Sidonians was blockading Tyre and preventing its inhabitants from securing vital supplies of fresh water, food and wood. Unable to defeat the Sidonian army, the Tyrian king, Abi-Milki (c. 1360-1310 BC), pleads for reinforcements from the Egyptian pharaoh. These letters reveal the extent of Tyre's dependence on Egypt for its commercial and military power during much of the eleventh century. Being the southernmost of the mainland Phoenician city-states, Tyre enjoyed, or indeed endured, a close commercial and political relationship with Egypt. In contrast, Sidon's commercial affinities meant that the city's political interests were orientated more towards Syria. The steady decline of Egypt as a market and profitable trade partner had a profound effect on Tyre, and perhaps best accounts for the city's precarious position throughout much of the eleventh century.

The tenth century BC

By the start of the tenth century the balance of power was beginning to shift away from Sidon and back to Tyre. Barely mentioned in the annals of the eleventh century, due largely to the perception that it was a satellite city of Sidon, Tyre quickly came to occupy a position of strength in its political dealings with the other Phoenician states. With the accession of Hiram I (969-936 BC), Tyre's golden age began, and from the tenth century onwards the history of Phoenicia largely becomes the history of Tyre. There can be little doubt that Tyre's dramatic change in fortune was the result of its systematic exploitation of pan-Mediterranean trade routes. The historical record clearly attests the city's burgeoning trade interests during the tenth century, in particular the period c. 971-939. The biblical book of Chronicles records that king Hiram skilfully achieved a monopoly over all maritime trade travelling up and down the Levantine coast. This account supports those sources which suggest that Hiram directly intervened in events on Cyprus (in particular to stifle an uprising of Kition), so that he could maintain tight control over the maritime trade routes into and out of the Levant. Such reports suggest that establishing commercial control of the eastern Mediterranean and Levantine coast was a key objective for Hiram. Through other biblical texts and from the writings of Flavius Josephus it is possible to identify that Tyre and Israel became close commercial allies during the tenth century. The biblical book 2 Chronicles states explicitly that king Hiram deliberately fostered a close commercial relationship with king Solomon of Israel (961-922 BC) in order to facilitate trade. As part of this commercial relationship the two states undertook a number of joint trading ventures in order to acquire gold from Ophir (the exact location of Ophir is unknown but it is believed to be either in Sudan or further south along the Eretrian-Somalian coast). Tyre's alliance with Israel also led to the creation and exploitation of a number of overland trade routes. This new network connected Tyre with those towns and cities founded in the interior of the continental Near East. Furthermore, Israel's dominance of the newly emerging Aramaean states in southern Syria facilitated overland communication with eastern Galilee, while granting access to the lucrative Transjordanian trade network. Finally, Israel's control of southern Judah coupled with king David's defeat of the Philistines gave Tyre access to the spices and precious metals of Southern Arabia. By the end of the tenth century, the successors of Hiram were to witness significant changes in the political climate of the Levant. These changes, including the division of Solomon's kingdom into two states, Judah and Israel, and the rise to prominence of the Aramaic states in the North, forced Tyre to re-evaluate its political alliances and joint commercial ventures.

The ninth century BC

The most successful ruler of Tyre in the ninth century was Ithobaal I (or Ethbaal, 887-856 BC) whose reign marked the beginning of a second 'golden age' for the city. During his reign the size of the territory controlled by Tyre increased dramatically, enabling Ithobaal to become the first king of Tyre to call himself 'king of the Sidonians', a title recorded in both the Old Testament and the poems of Homer. This title seems to have been adopted by the kings of Tyre as a direct consequence of Ithobaal's success in subjugating the southern regions of Phoenicia. In fact, Ithobaal achieved a feat of which none of his predecessors had been capable: the creation of a single state that embraced both Tyre and Sidon. This new confederacy, with Tyre as its capital and governed by Tyrian monarchs, lasted until the end of the eighth century BC. Ithobaal was also the first monarch credited with the foundation of Tyrian colonies, one at Auza in Libya and one at Botrys to the north of Byblos. The foundation of these colonies was the result of Tyre's commercial dominance over the Levant and came from a desire to exploit new sources of raw materials. Closer to home, Ithobaal established a colony at Kition on Cyprus in order to gain control of the island's lucrative copper trade.

Prior to the reign of Ashurnasirpal II, the Assyrian empire had not created any significant problems for the Phoenician city-states. Tyre had always managed to remain on the fringes of any armed conflict between Assyria and the states of western Asia, preferring to pay tribute rather than attempt to break free of Assyrian military control. Moreover, Tyre occasionally took advantage of the Assyrian campaigns in Mesopotamia to exploit the Mesopotamian monarchs' need for food and arms. However, the political situation changed dramatically when Ashurnasirpal's son, Shalmaneser III (858-824 BC), came to the throne and began an aggressive military campaign against northern Syria and southern Anatolia. The Assyrian annals record that he curtailed his campaign of conquest only once he had extracted tribute from 'the kings of the sea coast' (i.e. the Phoenician kings). On the bronze gates decorating Shalmeneser's palace at Dur-Sharrukin there is a frieze depicting the transport of Tyrian tribute to the Assyrian king. The tribute is carried by a long line of porters who are led into the presence of the Assyrian king and his court by two Tyrian dignitaries. The elderly figure of Ithobaal and his queen are shown watching these proceedings from the shores of Tyre's island capital (see Fig. 7).

Although the Phoenician city-states were now forced to pay an increased level of tribute and were more closely monitored than they had been before Shalmaneser's campaign, they still maintained their somewhat privileged position within the Assyrian empire, perhaps on account of their loyalty to, and commercial relationship with, Shalmaneser's father. In fact, the growing power of the Assyrian empire increased the Phoenician cities' geopolitical importance and enabled them to play a more prominent role in inter-regional politics and diplomacy. Their strategic position and economic importance meant they were a valuable resource which needed to be controlled in order to prevent them from falling into the political thrall of Assyria's great rival Egypt; yet they also needed to be allowed to flourish in order to help fill the coffers of the empire. Consequently, until the middle of the eighth century BC the Assyrian kings were content to collect tribute from the various Phoenician city-states while avoiding any direct interference which might harm their commercial interests. Shalmaneser's successors also avoided interfering in Phoenicia's internal affairs and governance, allowing the cities to maintain a limited level of independence.

The eighth and seventh centuries BC
Any pretence of Phoenician political independence was to come to an abrupt end with the ascension of Tiglath-Pileser III (744-727 BC) to the Assyrian throne. The recently crowned Assyrian monarch almost immediately initiated a series of wide-reaching campaigns aimed at the total conquest of the Levant and the annexation of all the various independent states. With the defeat of the northern Syrian kingdom of Unqi in c. 738 BC the whole of the Levant submitted to Assyrian authority. The cities of the northern Phoenician coast (i.e. all those north of Byblos) were directly annexed into a newly created Assyrian province. To the south, Tyre and Byblos were granted tributary status but kept under tighter control. In the following year, while Tiglath-Pileser was campaigning in the north, Tyre's king Hiram II (739-730 BC) chose to ally himself with an anti-Assyrian coalition (which included Syria, Israel and Philistia), and revolt from Assyrian rule. Tiglath-Pileser immediately responded to this threat: sweeping down the Phoenician coastline he quickly crushed any opposition to his rule. Tyre, following the lead of Arwad, immediately offered

its surrender to the Assyrian king and, although losing some of its territory, was in general treated leniently. This merciful treatment indicates that it was more important for Assyria to gain Tyre's economic cooperation than it was to punish the city for its insolence: a fact which reflects Assyria's inability to assume total control of Tyre's maritime trade networks. Tyrian commerce not only provided Assyria with access to vital resources, it also enabled Tyre to meet its tributary obligations, a vital source of income for the Assyrian state. Although not destroyed, Tyre paid a heavy price for its rebellion; the Assyrians installed inspectors and market officials in the city's harbours, removing any sense of economic or political freedom. The new king of Tyre, Mattan II (730-729 BC), was forced to pay 150 talents a year in tribute. This sum was the largest ever demanded from a Phoenician city and was intended to strip the Tyrians of both their wealth and their capacity to resist Assyria.

The beginning of king Elulaios' (also known as king Luli) reign in Tyre (729-694 BC) provided a brief respite from the conflict between Assyria and the coastal cities of Phoenicia. However, this respite did not last long as, having suppressed a number of rebellious allies, Elulaios adopted an anti-Assyrian stance. This led Tyre into a series of conflicts with Shalmaneser V (727-722 BC), Sargon II (722-705 BC) and Sennacherib (705-681 BC). Shalmaneser laid siege to Tyre for five years between 724-720 BC. During the siege he blockaded the city's port, cut off its water supplies and prevented the city from trading. Having forced the city into submission, Sargon did not merely annex its territories. Instead, he raised the stakes by initiating the policy of systematic destruction and mass deportations which he regularly implemented against other Phoenician cities. However, even Sargon shied away from the complete annihilation of Tyre. In 701 BC, Elulaios somehow managed to incur the wrath of Sennacherib who took vengeance by invading the outlying territories of Tyre. Realising he was finally out of options Elulaios fled to Cyprus where he lived out the rest of his days as an exile. His flight from Tyre seems to have averted the destruction of the city as the Assyrian annals make no mention of a siege.

The year 701 BC is, however, recognised as the end of the powerful unified state of Tyre and Sidon. Less than two years later Tyre had lost control of Sidon and the greater part of its mainland territories, while a large number of its citizen population was deported to Nineveh. By the beginning of the seventh century Tyre was a shadow of its former self, consisting solely of the city and its immediate suburbs on the mainland. Successive blockades by the Assyrian kings Esarhadon (681-671) in 671-667 BC and Ashurbanipal (668-626 BC) in 663 BC left the city more isolated than ever, and by 640 BC the entire mainland territory of Tyre had been turned into an Assyrian province. However, Assyrian dominance over the Levant was slowly beginning to falter and the campaign against Tyre was to be the last major Assyrian incursion into Phoenicia. Stuck in a debilitating war with Elam and plagued by civil unrest, the Assyrian empire was to become a victim of Babylonian expansionist policy. Moreover, the last quarter of the seventh century also saw a politically and militarily resurgent Egypt. Capitalising on the power vacuum left in the Levant, Egypt re-established its diplomatic ties with the north. This resulted in Tyre establishing a commercial enclave in Memphis, Egypt's capital. However, the Egyptians then took the ill-fated decision to ally themselves with their old enemy Assyria to try to check the threat of Babylon. In 605 BC the combined forces of Egypt and Assyria were defeated at Carchemish by a superior Babylonian force, a defeat that finally enabled Babylon to gain hegemony over the Levant.

The sixth and fifth centuries BC
In the first year of his reign the Babylonian king Nebuchadnezzar II (604-562 BC) undertook a series of campaigns in Syria during which he asserted his control over the whole region. Presented with another super-power, most of the Phoenician coastal cities duly submitted and offered tribute. Tyre, however, put up fierce resistance which resulted in Nebuchadnezzar undertaking a thirteen-year siege (585-572 BC) which ultimately had catastrophic repercussions for the city. As the prophet Ezekiel had forewarned, Tyre was reduced, at least in terms of political power, and the Tyrian king, Ithobaal III (591-573 BC), was deported to Babylon. His successor, Baal II (573-564 BC), was in essence a puppet ruler, and upon his death the system of monarchy in Tyre was replaced with a government of 'judges' under the authority first of Babylon and then of Persia (although monarchy was to be reintroduced at a later date). The conquest of Tyre by Babylon effectively ended the city's position of pre-eminence among the Phoenician city-states. During the remaining decades of the sixth century, Tyre's position at the head of a commercial empire was to be taken by its ancient rival Sidon. By usurping Tyre, Sidon became the most powerful and economically prosperous city in Phoenicia, continuing to hold this position until its capture by Alexander the Great. Generally, the Phoenician city-states suffered heavily under Babylonian rule and their commercial ventures diminished significantly. The Babylonian annexation of southern Palestine (Philistia, Judah and Samaria), Transjordan (Ammon and Moab), and Cilicia cut Phoenicia off from south Arabian and south Anatolian trade routes. More significantly, during the

reign of Nebuchadnezzar, the Babylonian state assumed control of Phoenicia's cherished cedar trade. Following the death of Nebuchadnezzar in 526 BC, Babylon began to lose its grip on Phoenicia. During the final years of Babylonian hegemony the Phoenician city-states seem to have enjoyed more independence as the Babylonian king Nabonidus (556-539 BC) was distracted by civil unrest at home. The reinstatement of the Tyrian dynastic line in 556 BC appears to have been a political gesture by Nabonidus aimed at ensuring the city's allegiance. It also seems that the exiled royal families of Sidon, Arwad and Byblos were reinstated as they make a sudden reappearance in the annals of the fifth century. This recognition of Phoenician autonomy by Nabonidus also best explains why the Phoenicians remained faithful to Babylon despite its waning power.

The decline of the Babylonian empire occurred quickly, the final death knell being sounded by Cyrus the Great's (559-530 BC) conquest of Sippar and then of the great city of Babylon itself. Cyrus seems to have treated the Phoenician city-states favourably, immediately recognising their strategic and commercial importance to his fledgling empire. Throughout most of Achaemenid history the Phoenicians served as the backbone of the Persian navy: on account of this willingness to provide naval assistance to the Persian king, the Phoenician cities were treated as allies rather than vassals. All the four major Phoenician city-states – Tyre, Sidon, Byblos and Arwad – were permitted to maintain their monarchic dynasties. In general, the Achaemenid era was a prosperous period in Phoenician history which saw the cities expand physically, through the development of urbanism, and in terms of their political and commercial influence. The Phoenician cities initially formed a satrapy (an administrative district) known as Athura ('Assyria') which also included all of Mesopotamia and Syria-Palestine. During the administrative reforms of Darius I (522-486 BC) the satrapy was subdivided and the Levantine regions west of the Euphrates became a separate province known as Abarnahara ('Beyond the River'). In terms of commercial enterprises Sidon is recorded as being at its most prosperous under the Persian empire. The Greek historian Diodorus highlights the wealth of the city and comments that the citizens of Sidon had amassed large fortunes due to their success at maritime trade. The high regard the Persians had for the Sidonian navy is best attested by the decision of Xerxes (485-465 BC) to travel aboard Sidonian galleys when on campaign (for more details see Chapter 6). The final years of the fifth century brought growing social and political unrest in Persia and saw the empire begin to fragment. The increasing independence of Egypt, western Asia Minor and mainland Greece was a cause of concern for the Phoenician city-states who relied on these regions as commercial partners. Thus, despite having remained loyal to the Persian empire throughout the fifth century, the Phoenicians, sensing the growing weakness of the Persian state, now turned their political and commercial attentions towards the western Mediterranean.

The fourth century BC

The first Phoenician state to demonstrate open hostility towards Persian rule was Tyre, which joined an anti-Persian alliance formed by Athens, Cyprus and Egypt. This decision may have been influenced by Tyre's long-standing commercial ties with both the Cypriots and the Egyptians. The Persians reacted decisively to this threat and in 381 BC they defeated the combined fleets of Tyre, Egypt and Cyprus. However, Achaemenid efforts to regain control of the Mediterranean border of its empire were on the whole ineffectual. In 373 BC Persia, utilising a fleet drawn from Phoenicia, Cyprus and Cilicia, launched a major offensive against Egypt. The campaign was a disaster and the Persians, having suffered heavy losses, were forced to withdraw. This failure to conquer Egypt proved an encouragement to other rebellious states and is often cited as one of the major catalysts for the so-called 'Great Satrapal Revolt' (363-361 BC). In 363 BC, having received military support from the Greek states and the Western Persian satrapies, the Egyptian Pharaoh Tachos (362-360 BC) undertook a campaign against Persian dominance in the Near East. The exact nature of the Phoenician participation in the revolt is unclear but Sidonian coinage suggests that the city nominally allied itself with Egypt. During the reign of Abdashart (365-352 BC), Sidonian coinage no longer displayed the standard motif of the kneeling Persian king; instead, it was stamped with a portrait of the Phoenician king resplendent in a royal crown. In 363/1 BC, with the revolt quelled, Sidon was occupied by a Persian garrison and placed under the authority of Mazaeus in recognition of his assistance in suppressing the rebellion. With the accession of Artaxerxes III Ochus (359/8-338/7 BC) Sidon became the centre of Persian efforts to re-establish control in the western empire. As part of this process the city was forced to billet large contingents of the Persian army, a situation that put considerable strain on the Sidonian economy. The Greek historian, Diodorus, records that relations between the Sidonians and the Persians became strained as the Persian officials taxed and requisitioned the city's resources with impunity. Thus, in 351 BC, less than ten years after the Great Satrapal Revolt, Sidon was again in open hostility with Persia. The recent defeat of the Persians by Egypt in the winter of 351/50 BC seems to have provided a catalyst for the Sidonian uprising, and also prompted rebellions by Arwad and Tyre. The contentious Persian officials

Fig. 5. Phoenician tribute bearers (?), Persepolis Frieze, *c.* fifth century BC (author's photo).

were all executed and the Persian royal game reserves near Sidon were ravaged. Bolstered by the presence of a large contingent of Greek mercenaries, the Sidonians succeeded in repelling the initial satrapal army dispatched by the Persian king, and the rebellion dragged on for several years. However, in 347 BC Sidon finally succumbed to the military might of Persia. The city apparently fell without a fight; distraught by the size of the Persian army (which classical sources record as numbering 300,000 men and a fleet of 800 warships and merchant vessels), the Phoenician king Tennes (351-347 BC) planned to betray the city to the Persians in exchange for his pardon and release. The result of Tennes' treachery was that 600 of Sidon's leading citizens were unwittingly lured into an ambush and massacred outside the city's gates. Diodorus records that many of the citizens choose to commit suicide rather than submit to the Persians. In total more than 40,000 people – men, women, children and household slaves – ended their own lives by immolation, sitting motionless as their houses burnt to the ground around them. Artaxerxes, determined to make an example of Sidon, is recorded as having ordered that the wealth of the city be collected from its smouldering ruins and sold to foreign merchants and traders. The surviving citizens were either deported or enslaved. Sidon's demise heralded the end of the revolt as the remaining Phoenician cities, stricken with fear, clamoured to make peace with the Persian king. Tennes, despite Artaxerxes' promises, was summarily executed and the city was once again placed under the rule of Mazaeus.

The conquest of the Persian empire by Alexander the Great (356-323 BC) marked the beginning of the end of Phoenicia as a Near Eastern entity. After the battle of Issus (333 BC), Alexander marched his victorious army along the Phoenician coastline. The cities of Arwad, Byblos and Sidon opened their gates to the conqueror and declared their fidelity. The fate of Tyre, however, was to be an entirely different story. When Alexander reached the gates of the city, king Azemilkos (Ozmilk, c. 350-333 BC), who was still in the service of the Persians, dispatched a high ranking princess to negotiate with the Macedonians in his stead. When Alexander demanded entry to the island fortress in order to offer sacrifices at the ancient temple of Heracles-Melqart, the princess countered with the suggestion that he might wish to offer libations at the even older temple to the god which was situated on the mainland. With an embassy from Carthage encouraging Tyre to resist, Azemilkos seems to have been trying to maintain Tyrian independence without upsetting the army on his doorstep. Alexander, however, was unwilling to give up the island fortress since it could be used as a base of resistance to Macedonian rule. The long-drawn-out siege, well documented in the classical sources, was to result in the island city being permanently joined to the mainland as a result of the mole Alexander constructed to bring his battering rams up against the city walls. Tyre fought doggedly, resisting both Alexander's siege and the blockade of its port by a fleet of Cypriot, Byblian and Sidonian vessels. Finally, after holding out for seven months, the city's defences were finally breached. Alexander, like Artaxerxes before him at Sidon, made an example of Tyre: he executed 6,000 citizens and sold a further 30,000 into slavery. As a reprisal for Tyre's earlier execution of Macedonian prisoners, Alexander also had 2,000 young men impaled on stakes and placed at regular intervals up and down the coast line. The intention was that their crucified bodies would serve as a stark reminder of the foolishness of opposing Macedon and the retribution that would follow any resistance. The age of Alexander marked the beginning of the Hellenistic period in the Eastern Mediterranean and the end of Phoenicia as a distinct state or province.

Chapter 3

The Phoenician Diaspora: Principal Cities and Colonies

One of the few constants in Phoenicia's turbulent history was the high population and settlement density found along its coastline. Phoenician towns and cities, whether trading posts, industrial settlements or urban centres, shared a number of characteristics. With few exceptions they were compact, easily defensible (most were protected by strong defensive walls), situated either directly on the coastline (on an islet lying just offshore) or near natural bays or harbours (sometimes river estuaries), and surrounded by a fertile hinterland that provided agricultural and mineral resources. They also shared a number of urban features which will be explored at greater length in Chapter 4. Due to the chance nature of archaeological discoveries, there is considerable variation in the knowledge and understanding of each site. Some, including Byblos, Tyre and Sidon, provide plentiful finds to help supplement the literary texts, whereas others, such as Kition and Carthage, both of which are known to have been important commercial centres in antiquity, have offered up significantly less material. This discontinuity in the historical record is the result of both the constant conflicts which have made large-scale excavation of many Phoenician cities impossible and the continued occupation or reuse of many of the sites. Subsequent building throughout the ages, from large Hellenistic and Roman cities down to crusader castles and Arab towns, has destroyed much of the earlier material, often eradicating whole centuries of history. For instance, in the case of Tyre, it is highly improbable that the world-famous 'Church of the Crusaders' will be torn down in order to grant classical archaeologists access to the equally famous temple of Melqart that lies underneath. These problems are compounded by a dearth of contemporary literary texts. Consequently, what follows is an overview of the pre-eminent cities and colonies of the Phoenician Diaspora that identifies their geographical location and provides a brief review of the literary and archaeological evidence pertaining to each.

Arwad

The city of Arwad was built on the largest of a chain of tiny islands extending south from Tortose (ancient Antarados) towards Tripoli. Oval in shape, the city measures only 800 x 500 m; as noted by Strabo, its surface area was so limited that houses had to be built several stories high. Although Arwad was occupied continuously from at least the third millennium BC, the city remains unexcavated and hence its urban history is virtually unknown. The site's name '*rwd*' means 'refuge' and appears in the Ebla archives as *A-ra-wa-ad*; in Akkadian as *Ar-wa-da* , *A-ru-da* or *A-ru-ad-da* in the Alalakh and Amarna tablets; as *Arados* in Greek and Latin; and as *Arwad* in Arabic. The name appears to have been derived from the fact that the city was served by a twin natural harbour that was well-sheltered and protected vessels from the violent storms that frequently swept the region. The island was first inhabited in the Neolithic period and saw continuous occupation until the Early Islamic period. The first literary reference to it is in the Amarna Letters which document that sailors from Arwad frequently travelled to Egypt and the eastern Mediterranean; while evidence contained in the annals of Tiglath-Pileser (1115-1077 BC) records that the continental area of Arwad provided food for the island and housed a large cemetery. At the beginning of the eighth century BC the city flourished as the result of its commercial and military shipbuilding industries. The skill and renown of Arwad's shipwrights meant the city was able to export, at considerable profit, a large volume of ships. In fact, shipbuilding is still a flourishing cottage industry on Arwad to this day. This lucrative revenue stream also enabled the city to expand its influence further inland. Furthermore, it is during the eighth century that the Greeks first established their settlements to the south of Arwad. In 701 BC, king Abdil'ti of Arwad was forced to pay tribute to the Assyrian king Sennacherib. Abdil'ti's successor, Matanaba'al, is mentioned among the twelve kings of the sea coast who were ordered by Esarhaddon to transport 'building materials' to Nineveh. Later administrative documents found in Babylon help to shed light on Arwad's political history as the city's king is recorded, among others, as 'belonging' to the court of Nebuchadrezzar II (605-562 BC). These documents also indicate that a number of skilled Arwadian carpenters lived and worked in the court of the Babylonian king. In the Persian period the Great King is known to have owned a lavish palace on the island while the Arwadian navy, led by Merbal son of Agbal, joined Xerxes' expedition against Greece. During Alexander's conquests of the Persian empire, Arwad's king, Gerastratos, surrendered the city to the Macedonian king. Later, however, Arwad was rewarded for its loyalty and granted autonomy by the Seleucids.

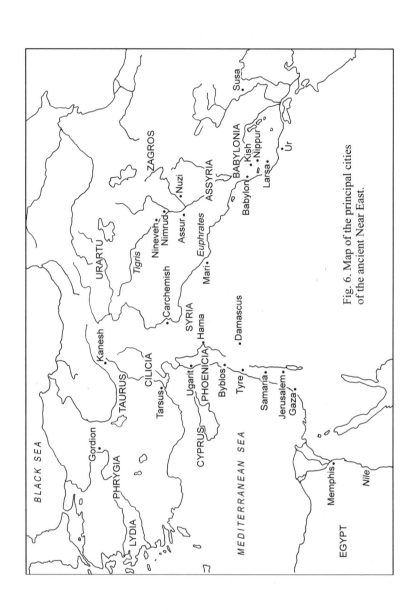

Fig. 6. Map of the principal cities of the ancient Near East.

Berytas

Berytas is the classical name for the ancient city of *Biruta*, modern Beirut. The name is generally believed to have been derived from the common Semitic word for 'well' or 'pit' – Akkadian *bŭrtu*, Hebrew *bě' ẑr* and Arabic *bûr*. Berytas was situated on a rocky promontory which had a deep, sheltered, natural harbour. Although kings from Egypt and Mesopotamia carved grand stelae into the rock cliffs at Nahr el-Kalb just north of the city, which recount their military exploits, written documents pertaining to the city's history are scant. For instance, neither Herodotus nor the Hebrew bible record its existence. However, the ancient city has now been revealed through archaeological research undertaken as part of the redevelopment of war-torn Beirut. During the early nineties, an international archaeological team, funded by the Lebanese Department of Antiquities and UNESCO, carried out a series of archaeological rescue operations aimed at exploring and preserving the evidence from the outer limits of the ancient town. With the site under threat from developers, the project aimed to rescue precious artefacts and document as much of the site as possible before it was cleared for construction. Due to the limited time available, its organisers chose to focus their efforts on recovery rather than systematic cataloguing and publication, and thus many of the project's finds are still unpublished.

The excavations revealed that Berytus was occupied from at least the mid-Bronze Age when the site was first fortified and equipped with a monumental gate. The original settlement occupied an oval tell of roughly 5 acres. To the west of the modern city archaeologists unearthed a residential district which contained well-preserved dwellings built using the pier-and-rubble technique and laid out in an orthogonal arrangement. In the area just to the north-west, a large quantity of murex shells and a basin complex have been discovered, both of which are indicative of purple-dye production. The close proximity of both districts to the city's harbour reveals their commercial focus. The excavations also revealed that during the Hellenistic period Berytas underwent extensive urban development which had begun in the third century under the Seleucids. As with so many Phoenician sites, much of the material evidence pertaining to the daily lives of the citizens survives in a funerary context. For instance, archaeologists working in what was believed to be the city's main port district recovered an Egyptian sphinx bearing a royal inscription of Amenemhet IV. Just north of the sphinx, three tombs were discovered containing burials of seventeenth- and sixteenth-century date. They contained a variety of ceramic artefacts including metal tools, Egyptian scarabs and alabaster vases, all of which point to a flourishing trade network and a close relationship with Egypt. A fourth tomb, dating to the late Bronze Age, was found to contain Cypriot and Mycenaean pottery, suggesting that the city also had trade connections in the Aegean.

Byblos

Byblos is a seaport located on the eastern coast of the Mediterranean at the foot of the Lebanese mountains some 60 km north of Beirut. The site has been known throughout history by a variety of names including in modern Arabic *Jebail, Jebeil, Jubail*; by the crusaders as *Gibelete*; in biblical Hebrew as *Gebal*, in Egyptian as *kbn, kpny, kbny*, and in Babylonian as *Gubla*. However, it appears that it was the Greeks who gave the city the name 'Byblos', most likely at the end of the second century BC, as it is derived from the Greek word *bublos*, 'papyrus scroll'. This is significant as it is known that Egyptian papyrus first came to Greece through Phoenicia, and that traders from Byblos specialised in the export of this commodity. Indeed, the English word *Bible* is derived through medieval Latin from the Greek *ta biblia*, 'the books'.

Philo of Byblos records that during antiquity the city was thought to be the oldest in the world, while according to other classical traditions, Byblos was founded by Cronus at the location where the god Thoth was believed to have invented writing. Archaeology has now shown that the site of Byblos was first settled during the Neolithic period and became a permanent settlement sometime during the third millennium BC, supporting Philo's claims for the longevity of the city. The site appears to have been chosen because of the ease of access to water: archaeologists have uncovered a large rock-cut well in the centre of the city which would have provided the population with plentiful supplies of clean, fresh water. The city was also close to a source of copper and to abundant tracts of cedar trees that grew on the adjacent mountain slopes; most importantly, though, the site was chosen because it was on the coast. This enabled the Byblians to exploit a variety of maritime commercial opportunities, and the city quickly became wealthy. Consequently, by the Early Bronze Age Byblos had already become an important trading emporium which connected Canaan and Egypt with the wider Mediterranean world: a fact attested by the annals of Tiglath-Pileser I, the *Report of Wen-Amon* and the Egyptian text of Thutmose III. Archaeological excavations have confirmed that throughout its history the city continued to be an important commercial emporium. During a series of digs spanning more than 50 years, archaeologists have uncovered three distinct port districts: two small harbours located just to the north of the main acropolis, and a much larger harbour in the city's southern district. The two smaller harbours are far too shallow to have moored larger vessels, so archaeologists conclude that the larger and deeper southern harbour must have been the maritime heartland of the city. This theory would also account for the city's expansion along the eastern coastal plain. Byblos' principal settlement was sited on an elevated circular tract of land of *c.* 7 acres. There is evidence from as early as 2800 BC suggesting that Byblos was a planned city, but the superimposition of remains and the upheaval caused by the construction of large buildings in the Roman period have made it difficult to trace the development of the early settlement. Surviving material remains indicate that the early settlement expanded rapidly, especially after 2700 BC when the city first began fostering trade relations with Egypt. Although an Amorite invasion destroyed Byblos between *c.* 2300 and 2100 BC, a new wave of settlers re-founded the city in *c.* 2000. Once again the city is believed to have rapidly expanded, a hypothesis supported by ongoing archaeological investigations which have revealed a number of well-built houses dating to the middle Bronze Age. These houses are all of uniform shape and size, and are constructed from a mixture of materials including stone blocks, mud bricks, wooden facing, and mud plaster. The Bronze Age also saw the city surrounded by a circuit of high walls. These were breached by two large gateways: one was approached from the east, and the other provided access from the large harbour district just to the south of the city. From the beginning of the ninth century BC, the city walls received constant attention and were regularly strengthened (particularly the southern gate). Building activity peaked during the Persian period when the city became a regional administrative centre for the Persian empire. In fact Byblos was so prosperous that king Yehawmilk (*c.* 450 BC) was able to restore a number of the city's public buildings while simultaneously spending lavish amounts on the ancient sanctuary of Baalath. The substantial contributions made by Yehawmilk to the temple of Baalath are recorded on a commemorative inscription accompanied by a relief depicting the king standing before the seated goddess in the pose of a devoted gift-bearer. In 333-323 BC, Alexander the Great conquered the Phoenician coastline and Byblos willingly became part of the Macedonian empire. After the conquest of Antiochus III in 200 BC the city became completely Hellenised, and by 64 BC it had lost much of its political power and influence.

Sarepta

Thanks to the discovery of a series of inscriptions written in the Phoenician script, the ancient city of Sarepta has been securely located to a site in south Lebanon near the modern city of Sarafand. The name Sarepta seems to derive from the Semitic root *saraph* or *sarapu*, meaning 'to refine' or 'to colour red', an interpretation supported by the discovery of 22 stone-built pottery-kilns, slip basins and tanks for washing and storing clay. The presence of industrial sized workshops is often indicative of red-slip pottery manufacture, an industry for which Sarepta was particularly famed. Its other main industries included purple-dye production, metalworking and cash-crop farming (especially olive production). The only written texts thus far discovered in Sarepta are 21 inscriptions: these vary in length from a single Phoenician character to a text containing all 32 Phoenician letters inscribed on a votive dedication to the goddess Tanit. Although there are few extant documents from the city itself, the history of Sarepta can be pieced together from references in more than 50 ancient texts: these include the fourteenth-century Ugaritic texts, a number of thirteenth-century Egyptian papyri, the eighth-century Assyrian annals and the biblical book of Kings which records that the prophet Elijah visited Sarepta and performed two miracles (1 Kings 17:8-28). The biblical account also documents that during the reign of Ahab (874-853 BC), the city was subject to the rule of the Sidonians.

In typical Phoenician fashion Sarepta was constructed on a low mound located on the shore of the Mediterranean Sea, a position which ensured the city could maintain undisrupted access to the sea. The site of the ancient city is marked by two sets of ruins just to the south of the modern town. The ruins are in two distinct groups: the first are on a headland just to the west of a fountain known as 'Ain el-Kantara' and are part of the port district; the second group is to the south and consists of columns, sarcophagi and marble slabs which indicate the presence of a sizeable city. Sarepta was the first Iron Age site in mainland Phoenicia to receive sustained attention from archaeologists. Excavations of the southern district during the 1960s revealed many artefacts and buildings associated with everyday life, including a pottery (with kilns), a stonemason's workshop, votive offerings such as figurines and amulets, seal stones, and a number of fragmentary inscriptions. Perhaps the most significant discovery was a sanctuary dedicated to Tanit-Astarte, which archaeologists believe was in use during the eighth to seventh centuries. An inscription, recovered from inside the temple, records an offering made by a devotee to the goddess Tanit, a deity whom scholars had previously believed was worshipped only by the Carthaginians. The excavations also revealed that the transition from the Bronze to the Iron Age had been relatively peaceful for Sarepta as there was no evidence of any widespread destruction. As a consequence, the city's economy flourished, enabling Sarepta's manufacturing and commercial sectors to expand rapidly. This may account for the two harbours flanking the city to the north and south, particularly well-preserved with a number of mooring stations and structures still surviving.

Sidon

The port city of Sidon (or *Saida* in Arabic) is located 43 km south of Beirut. Its name is probably derived from the Semitic word *sayd*, 'fishing'. Sidon was inhabited from approximately 4000 BC, with some scholars suggesting that the site may even have been occupied during the Neolithic period. Since each successive occupation of the ancient city has involved building over the previous foundations, a systematic reconstruction of the site has not been possible. However, much of Sidon's history can be carefully reconstructed from various literary sources, and from the material record generated by archaeological excavation of the city and its hinterland. For example, in Greek literature, Homer can be found praising the skills of Sidonian craftsmen who produced glass, textiles and dyes, industries which are also well attested in the archaeological record.

The city is situated on a small promontory bordered by a line of reefs which protect the two natural harbours adjacent to the city. Due to a number of extensive archaeological and topographical surveys, it has been possible to construct a general outline of the city and its suburbs. The heartland of the city's territory consisted of a narrow, fertile, well-hydrated agricultural plain, but Sidon also controlled a hinterland that extended into the eastern foothills of the Lebanon Mountains and beyond. The surveys also revealed that Sidon's oval tell was divided longitudinally into two distinct regions: a low lying district to the east and an elevated coastal region to the west. The western district of the city housed the residences of the elite and appears to have served as the administrative quarter; the eastern half was devoted to industry and manufacture. Although as yet undiscovered, it is likely that a palace or fortress stood on the summit of the largest hill in the western district. To the south of this acropolis is a circular cove which is still littered with discarded murex shells (in some places piled up to 40 m high). The cove, which was too shallow to serve as the city's main harbour, seems to have been used as an area for offloading the shallow-hulled fishing vessels that provided the dyeing industry with regular supplies of murex.

Archaeological excavations of the city's hinterland have revealed a large number of tombs which have helped to illuminate Phoenician burial practices and eschatological beliefs. For instance, the necropolis at Dakerman, a coastal cemetery located just to the south of the city, has yielded several hundred tombs dating between the mid-fourteenth century and the early Roman period. A large number of Bronze Age and early to mid-Iron Age burial sites have also been located further inland. Ongoing excavations have also revealed a sanctuary precinct dedicated to Eshmun, indicating that large-scale ritual activity was not confined to the city. The site was constructed over a series of split levels and was originally built in the sixth century and then restored or rebuilt in subsequent periods. Further evidence for the extensive territory controlled by Sidon is found on an inscribed prism dating to the time of the Assyrian king Sennacherib (704-681 BC). This document records that Sidon controlled a considerable number of satellite towns and villages, the most prominent of which was Sarpeta. The inscription also records that many of these towns were walled fortresses that stored provisions for the Sidonian military and served as the first line of defence against invaders. During the Persian period, Sidon was the seat of a Persian governor whose palace seems to have been built in typical Achaemenid fashion: a fact attested by the discovery of a column capital carved in the form of twin bulls' heads. This motif has clear parallels with the column capitals found at the Persian palace at Persepolis.

Tyre

Tyre was located on two sandstone reefs about 2 km off the coast of South Lebanon, but virtually every trace of the ancient city has been eliminated. Classical tradition suggests that king Hiram connected the two reefs with landfill, thus enlarging the city to approximately 40 acres. During the reigns of succeeding kings, further enlargement allowed the creation of ports on the northern and southern sides of the island. Because of Tyre's extended urban history, it seems unlikely that there was much opportunity for centralised planning except, perhaps, in the newly developed regions around the city's outskirts. Archaeological evidence has suggested that the Tyrians often reused the limited building materials at their disposal. Tyre's current physical location is vastly different from that of the ancient city. The headland on which it stands is the consequence of successive sediment deposits that built up around the causeway constructed by Alexander the Great in 332 BC. By Roman times, the sand deposited by the fast moving currents that surround the island had quickly enveloped the causeway, creating the present isthmus. Although the site was originally settled in the Early Bronze Age, after a relatively brief period of habitation of c. 500 years it was abandoned and not resettled until the sixteenth century BC. The material record suggests that permanent settlement of the island did not occur until the end of the fifteenth century BC.

During the late Bronze Age, references to Tyre can be found in

Fig. 7. Bronze band from the palace gates of Shalmaneser III showing the king receiving tribute from Tyre and Sidon (courtesy of the British Museum).

Egyptian, Assyrian, Persian and Babylonian documents, all of which attest to the city's importance as a major commercial entrepôt. Herodotus, who is believed to have visited Tyre in the mid-fourth century BC, reports, on the authority of local priests, that the city had been founded some 2,300 years previously, i.e. *c.* 2750 BC. Whether by coincidence, or because of accurate records maintained in the city's archives, this date closely corresponds to those proposed by archaeologists. However, due to the construction projects undertaken by king Hiram I (969-936 BC), evidence for the earliest settlement has been erased. By the fourth century the city of Tyre was densely populated: Arrian records that the population had reached approximately 40,000, while Strabo claims that, due to severe overcrowding and lack of space, the Tyrians were forced to construct a number of public and private multi-storeyed buildings.

During the reign of Hiram I, the ground in the eastern part of the settlement was levelled through the use of artificial earthen mounds, and the main section of the city was connected to an adjoining islet by the construction of a causeway. Archaeologists have drawn cautious conclusions about the general location of the city's major landmarks and civic features, but Josephus and Herodotus tell us that the main temple of Melqart, built by Hiram, was situated on the most northerly, and largest, of Tyre's islands. Archaeologists have therefore suggested, albeit tentatively, that this may equate to the island sanctuary of Baal Shamen. Herodotus states that the temple was renowned in antiquity for its twin columns: one of emerald and one of gold. A lesser temple of Melqart, which is believed to have been directly adjacent to a temple of Astarte, is now thought to have been situated on the mainland. Justin and Curtius Rufus claim that this temple was even more ancient than the one built by Hiram. Tyre's other great monumental structure was its city walls. Owing to a pressing need for security, Tyre seems to have been heavily fortified from as early as the ninth century BC. The strength of the city walls is evident from the Balawat gates which depict the city surrounded by a multi-storeyed circuit wall that included regularly spaced towers and large arched gateways. According to classical sources, by the fourth century BC the walls of Tyre were *c.* 45 m high. The reconstructed fortification revealed by excavations in the late 1980s belongs to the Persian period and includes a double set of stone walls 4 m thick. Another prominent feature of the city was its system for collecting water. Whereas prior to the early Iron Age water had to be ferried over from the mainland, after *c.* 1250 BC the Tyrians collected and stored rainwater in large cisterns waterproofed with lime plaster. The eastern section of the city contained Tyre's large-scale manufacturing industries, including metal foundries, textile dyeworks, fisheries and tanneries, all of which produced foul smells and needed to be located away from the city. The smaller cottage industries, such as weaving, pottery production and jewellery manufacturing, seem to have occurred throughout the city.

Although Tyre was an island city, it was dependent on the mainland for natural resources, especially food, water and fuel. Its mainland territory was located within a narrow coastal stretch of land extending from the River Litani in the north to the promontory of Ras en-Naqura to the south. The focus of Tyre's mainland interests was the town of Ushu (known in the classical sources as *Palaetyrus*, or ancient Tyre), which served as the city's main dependency and provided it with raw materials and water. Ushu also provided Tyre with a base of operations for its southwards expansion into the fertile Akko Plain and Northern Galilee. The various cemeteries uncovered on the mainland directly east of Tyre have provided an insight into the extent of the territory controlled by the city. Cemeteries at Tell Rachidiyeh, Joya and Qasmieh indicate that Tyre had a flourishing rural population which must have supplied the city with vital agricultural and mineral resources.

Carthage
Carthage (*Karkhêdôn* in Greek; *Carthago* in Latin) is located on the North African coastline and is now a suburb of modern Tunis. Classical sources agree that the city was a colony originally founded by Tyre, and most ancient sources place the founding of the city in *c.* 814-813 BC. According

to Dionysius of Halicarnassus, the traditional date for the foundation of Carthage was considered to be 38 years before the first Olympiad, i.e. 814 BC, a date which he claims was recorded by an earlier historian, Timaeus. This date is also posited by Josephus, who claims to have used the work of Menander, a historian who Josephus believed had access to the Tyrian royal annals and was therefore trustworthy. The Roman historian Velleius Paterculus, discussing Carthage's fall in 146 BC, assigns it 667 years of recorded history: this again makes the foundation date 814 BC. For many years the dates provided by the ancient writers were considered to be inaccurate as they were not borne out by the results of archaeological excavations, all of which pointed towards a much later date for the city's foundation. But in the late 1990s it became clear that although the archaeologists had been thorough, their method of dating was fundamentally incorrect. Essentially they had derived all their dates from the pottery evidence: this was done by studying the raw material used in manufacture, the process of forming or moulding, the colours applied, the style or shape, any patterns or inscriptions, the firing method and, finally, any wear or usage marks. Once a style or type of pottery had been analysed, it was placed into an approximate sequence alongside previously studied items; this provided a rough date for when the object was manufactured and subsequently deposited. Although it was recognised that these dates were problematic, it was not until the 1990s, when radiocarbon dating was first applied to the finds from Carthage, that archaeologists realised their mistake. The results of this more scientific analysis revealed that the oldest finds in Carthage could now be dated to the last quarter of the ninth century, or *c*. 814 BC.

According to legend, Carthage was founded by the Tyrian Queen Elissa, later known to classical authors as Dido. The city was originally called Qart Hadasht ('new town') and its people continued to honour Tyre for centuries after its foundation. This involved sending annual offerings from the first fruits as dedications to the main religious sanctuaries in Tyre. The Phoenician ancestry of Carthage is also reflected in the Latin term *Punicus*, which is an adjectival derivation from the Greek for 'Phoenician'. The term 'Punic' is now used to designate anything relating to Carthage. Unfortunately, due to the Roman sacking of the city in 146 BC, the dispersal of the city's libraries, and the clearing of the site by Augustus when founding his colony 'New Carthage', no Punic literature survives. Moreover, despite there being references to Carthage in the works of more than 40 Greek and Latin authors, these must be treated with caution. The loss of Carthage's literary texts is to some extent compensated by the survival of a large quantity of inscriptions: Carthage itself has yielded over 6,000, while other North African and Western Mediterranean sites have added approximately 1,000 more. Most of these are simple formulaic votive offerings or epitaphs but some are more substantial documents which can be used, in particular, to illuminate Carthaginian religious practices.

Carthage is perhaps most famous for its extensive trading interests and the fierce wars it fought in order to defend them. Even in the early sixth century the Carthaginians were contesting the foundation of non-Punic colonies in regions where they had a commercial interest. By the fourth century Carthage had become a major commercial and political power: it struck gold and silver coinage, imported pottery and luxury goods from Greece, and exported its own manufactured goods and surplus agricultural produce throughout the Mediterranean. The urban development of Carthage has been well-documented due to a number of large-scale archaeological excavations. The UNESCO-sponsored projects, which were undertaken with the aim of 'saving Carthage', revealed that the earliest city lay between the Byrsa hill and the sea; occupation sequences for this region can be dated as far back as the first quarter of the eighth century. Finally, recent excavations have corroborated Appian's description of the city and have indicated that the two harbours were constructed during the second century. If this date is correct then it means the harbours were built in direct violation of the peace treaty signed with Rome at the end of the Second Punic War.

Gades

The ancient Tyrian colony of Gades is located directly under the site of the historical centre of modern Cadiz on the small island of San Sebastian. According to descriptions offered by classical authors, the main island was long and thin and terminated in a promontory at each end. The city is well-documented in antiquity and a number of classical sources try to establish the colony's foundation date. Strabo (quoting Posidonius), suggests that the Tyrians sent out various expeditions to prospect for metal and it was as a direct consequence of these voyages that Gades was founded. Velleius Paterculus specifies that it was 80 years after the sack of Troy (c. 1104-1103 BC) that the Phoenicians first established a settlement at Gades. Diodorus, on the other hand, suggests that Gades was founded by a group of Tyrian merchants who, having been blown off course, sought shelter and discovered the site. Despite their differing methods of 'careful calculation' and 'meticulous research', the dates proposed by all the ancient authors are wildly inaccurate: archaeology has now conclusively shown that the indigenous tribes of the Gades region did not receive Phoenician imports until the years 760-750 BC. This is a decisive argument against the hypothesis that Gades was founded before the eighth century. The primary texts are also doubtful in the reasons they give for the founding of the colony: all propose that the site was deliberately colonised because of its close proximity to various mineral resources, including silver, gold, copper and tin. These metals could either be sold in their raw form or worked and sold on as luxury items. Diodorus claims that the Phoenicians grew so rich from the trade in Spanish metals that they were able to found a number of colonies throughout the Mediterranean. Although mineral wealth was undoubtedly one of the major factors which prompted the colonisation of Gades, it was not the only one. Archaeology has shown that commerce, agriculture and industry were also important stimuli for the Phoenician colonisation of Southern Spain: a hypothesis supported by Strabo who praises the region for being uniquely blessed with both mineral resources and great natural fertility. Therefore, just as with Greek colonisation, which should not be seen simply as a way to relocate surplus population, Phoenician objectives for founding new cities were varied and changed according to local conditions.

Gades was located on the western promontory of the island, while the renowned temple of Hercules-Melqart was constructed on the eastern. The construction of the shrine occurred at the same time as the foundation of the colony suggesting that, in the minds of the colonists at least, the deity had sanctioned their city and would watch over its well-being and interests. The fame and prestige of this temple was considerable and remained so until the medieval period. The temple had no images or visual representations of the god, a circumstance which surprised many ancient authors. Aside from the lack of cult image, the Greek historian Arrian informs us that both the architecture and the sacrificial rites of the temple reflected its Phoenician origins. This is confirmed by Appian, Silius Italicus and Diodorus, who all stress the temple's great antiquity and sumptuousness. The Phoenician-Punic city remained relatively small until the Roman period; Gades, however, was not limited to a few islands close to the mainland. The position of the city also allowed it to dominate an important inlet which provided access to the Guadalquivir, a river which served as the main line of communication for the whole of Lower Andalusia. The Guadalquivir was also used to transport the mineral resources from the interior of Spain to the coast where they could be shipped throughout the Mediterranean. Consequently, the colony was in a prime location to monopolise the metal trade. A recent study of the Tartessian Orientalising period highlights the skill with which the Phoenicians interacted with the native inhabitants of the regions they colo-

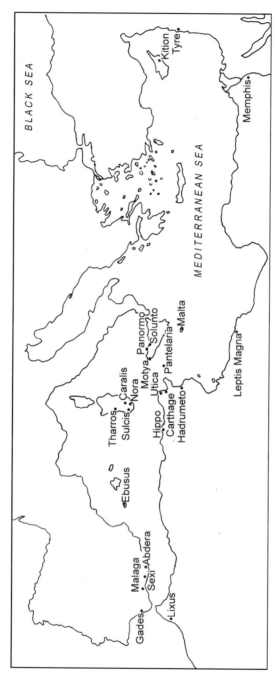

Fig. 8. Map of Phoenician colonies and emporia across the Mediterranean.

nised. In exchange for prestigious gifts and luxurious items – ivory, jewellery, metal bowls – which the indigenous tribal leaders used for their sumptuous burials, the Phoenicians were granted the right of transit to interior territories with silver deposits and fertile agricultural land. The large volume of imported Phoenician pottery, which first appears in interior settlements during the 750s and 740s BC, suggests a relatively rapid extension of Gades' commercial networks. In the Punic era, Gades continued to maintain close ties with the east, despite the fact that Tyre broke off its trading connections with the Tartessians. Especially close connections were maintained with Sidon whence the wealthy citizens of Gades purchased the valuable anthropomorphic sarcophagi they used to decorate their tombs.

Kition

Kition – *Kt(y)* in Phoenician; *Kit(i)on* in Greek, and *Citium* in Latin – is located below the modern city of Larnaka on the southeast coast of Cyprus. The ancient territory of the Cypro-Phoenician kingdom of Kition was bordered by the sea to the south and southwest, the territories of Salamis to the northwest, and Amathus to the west. The earliest Phoenician occupation of Kition occurred during the early Bronze Age and is clearly attested in the funerary record. Recent excavations have shown that by the end of the Bronze Age, Kition was flourishing; however, during the course of the eleventh century the city was destroyed and subsequently rebuilt. The newly rebuilt city was occupied for only 50 years before it was again abandoned due, at least partially, to the silting up of its harbour. During the ninth century an artificial harbour was excavated just to the south of the old natural anchorage: a new Phoenician town quickly grew up around it. As it flourished, its suburbs expanded to include the site of the old city, and by the end of the ninth century the region was densely populated.

Kition is well documented in both literary texts and inscriptions, especially of the fifth and fourth centuries, and is recorded as being an important source of copper. Inscriptions and the legends on coins preserve the name of several kings of Kition including Baalmilk I, Azibaal, and Baalmilk II in the fifth century, and Milkyaton and Pumayyaton in the fourth century. The city's affluence depended on maritime trade, and it developed and maintained a large naval force. The city used this navy to involve itself in the ongoing rivalry between Greece and Persia, and in the prevalent regional conflicts fought between the Phoenician cities of the Levant. Recent excavations have uncovered a portion of the city's extensive dockyards, which seem to have been constructed at the end of the fifth century at the height of Kition's wealth and prestige. The most famous citizen of Kition was Zeno, founder of the Stoic school of philosophy, who was born in the city sometime during the early fourth century. By 315 BC Kition had been subjugated by the Egyptian Pharaoh Ptolemy I Soter and was slowly being Hellenised. However, Cicero records in *De Finibus* that despite these Hellenising influences Kition still retained some of its Phoenician character.

Motya

Motya (*Motua* in Greek or *Mothia* in Latin) is a Phoenician colony located on an island just off the west coast of Sicily, between Drepanum (modern Trapani) and Lilybaeum (modern Marsala). The Phoenician interest in Sicily arose from the island's position at the crossroads of a number of important Mediterranean trade routes. Thucydides tells us that when the Greeks started to colonise Sicily in the eighth century, the Phoenicians, who already occupied the main coastal promontories and islands, were forced (or perhaps agreed) to withdraw to the western end of the island. Having abandoned a number of their original colonies, the Phoenicians now founded three new cities: Motya, Panormo and Solunto, of which Motya was undoubtedly the most important. Because Motya was inhabited without interruption from the end of the eighth to the middle of the fourth century BC, the city is one of the best-documented Phoenician colonies. Until 650 BC the area assigned to dwellings was relatively small, as was the resident population, a hypothesis supported by the discovery of Motya's main cemeteries. The number of burials in these cemeteries has shown that, prior to the seventh century BC, the population density of the city remained low. However, from the middle of the seventh century, there is a sudden increase in the number of burials which archaeologists have suggested was the result of a sudden rise in population. This growth was to reach its peak in the sixth century when there were approximately 15,800 inhabitants.

Due to the city's commercial interests, its citizens constructed a number of mercantile harbours around the edges of the island. Excavations undertaken by the British Museum in the mid to late 1980s demonstrated that, in addition to a *cothon* (dry dock), the island was also served by an extensive harbour complex comprising the whole of Stagnone and a series of smaller ports dotted around its coastline. Moreover, the discovery of a number of large industrial complexes proved that, by the seventh century, Motya had developed a number of specialised industries, such as iron working and dye production, both of which were manufacturing commodities for export. During the sixth century the Motyans redeveloped their urban centre and constructed a number of monumental public buildings, including the *temenos* (sacred enclosure) at the sanctuary of Cappidazzu, a fully enclosed harbour, extensive city walls, and a causeway linking Motya to mainland Sicily. Although Motya began life as a small trade emporium, it gradually expanded into a flourishing and geopolitically important town. Motya's location provided the city with two significant advantages: first, it enabled the Motyans to form a powerful alliance with the Elymians who occupied a number of sites in western Sicily; secondly, it enabled the city to foster close links with Carthage that was located on the other side of the Sicilian straits. These factors enabled Motya to gain prominence over the other Phoenician colonies on Sicily; however, this situation came to an end with the accession of Dionysius I of Syracuse (432-367 BC), who besieged Motya in 397 BC. After its eventual capture, the city never recovered its former glory and by the time of the Roman invasion of Sicily during the First Punic War, Motya had been eclipsed by the Carthaginian colony, Lilybaeum.

Utica

The colony of Utica was founded as a harbour city located close to a series of trade routes leading from the Straits of Gibraltar and the Atlantic into the eastern Mediterranean. It is 40 km to the northwest of Carthage and was intentionally founded with a view to exploiting the numerous trade networks that hugged the North African coast. The monumental architecture of Utica's graveyards and the opulent foreign grave goods found in its cemeteries suggest that the city's citizens had grown wealthy through commerce. This theory is supported by the fact that Utica, like its neighbour Carthage, does not appear to have developed a substantial agricultural infrastructure during its early years. The exact foundation date of Utica is still widely debated: several classical authors date it to around 1100 BC, while the archaeological record indicates a date no earlier than the eighth century BC. Interestingly, during the sixth century there is still no mention of Utica involving itself in the main political events of the day. This would seem to indicate that the city maintained a low profile in an effort to maintain its political independence. By the fourth century Utica had come under Carthaginian control but was granted the status of 'privileged ally' rather than vassal state. This situation was to continue until the Mercenary War (c.240 BC) when Utica abandoned its allegiance to Carthage and instead offered its support to the disgruntled mercenaries. The city was besieged by the Carthaginians and rapidly subjugated. Although Carthage regained control of Utica it was not treated particularly harshly and thus relations between the two cities remained fairly cordial until the destruction of Carthage during the Third Punic War.

Chapter 4

Government and Society

It is difficult to speak with certainty about the governance of Phoenician cities and the various political and administrative infrastructures that regulated the daily lives of the Phoenicians, as, unfortunately, there are no surviving documents written by the Phoenicians themselves. Instead, historians are mainly reliant on the accounts of later western authors, or on comparisons drawn with the better documented institutions found in Carthage. Despite the dearth of literary texts, it is possible to ascertain that throughout much of their history the Phoenician cities remained politically independent of each other, each looking out for its own individual interests while controlling a clearly defined territory from which it took agricultural and mineral resources. Although some of the major cities such as Sidon and Tyre gained hegemony over the other city-states, at least for short periods, there was never a Phoenician confederacy, still less a Phoenician 'nation'. This lack of unity perhaps makes it more surprising that so many of the Phoenicians cities managed to become commercial power-houses. Institutionally, then, the Phoenician towns functioned as true city-states, each operating with full autonomy under the auspices of a local monarch. However, when examining the governments and political infrastructures found in each of the Phoenician city-states, it is worth remembering that for much of their history they were vassals of a more powerful empire. Egypt, Assyria, Babylon, Persia and Macedonia all ruled Phoenicia at different times and the political independence of each city varied dramatically under these regimes. Although in general foreign overlords followed a relatively non-invasive policy, the Phoenician city-states were nevertheless subject to the will of foreign tax collectors, governors and generals.

Monarchy

The institution of monarchy was present in some form in all the Phoenician cities, and, for most, monarchic rule was an early development. In Tyre, for instance, the monarchic tradition began during the first half of the nineteenth century BC and continued until the destruction of the city at the hands of Alexander the Great. Judging by the system in Tyre, the

Phoenician monarchies were hereditary, with inter-marriage between family members a common practice. Such marriage arrangements were designed to help avoid disputed successions, and to prevent the kingship from passing to another powerful family. Information about the structure and importance of the monarchic tradition in the Phoenician city-states is scarce; unlike other Near Eastern monarchies the Phoenician kings did not, as far as is known, record their exploits on public inscriptions and reliefs. Historians therefore lack the propaganda that was so prevalent in other contemporary societies, such as Assyria and Egypt, and which can provide unique insights into a state's political organisation. The only surviving commemorative inscriptions are those found in the royal tombs of Byblos and Sidon; even these are of limited use with many recording little more than the monarch's name and a brief outline of his achievements. Although we know little about the powers of the kings, the surviving evidence does indicate that their rule was absolute. This can certainly be inferred from the behaviour of Hiram I, Ithobaal or Eulaios of Tyre. Comparisons between the political activities of the Phoenician kings and their counterparts in other Near Eastern societies reveal little difference in patterns of behaviour. Hiram I expressed his monarchical power through the construction of a lavish new royal palace. The construction of a palace is often indicative of a ruler with absolute power; typically in oligarchies, or in states ruled by a more limited form of monarchy, political statements were made through the construction of 'public' amenities such as temples, markets or city walls, rather than through more 'personal' monumental buildings such as palaces. Further evidence for absolute monarchy is contained in the account of Wen-Amon. In this text, the local dynast, Zakarbaal, is depicted as an aggressive and vigorous monarch who was directly involved in matters of state. In his dealings with Wen-Amon, Zakarbaal managed all aspects of the cedar trade, from the initial business negotiations and contract of sale to the appointment of woodsmen to cut down and transport the timber.

The correspondence with the monarchies in Tyre, Byblos and Sidon, contained in the Amarna Letters, indicates by its language, tone and content that by the fourteenth century the largest Phoenician city-states were ruled by a form of absolute monarchy. As in other Near Eastern monarchies, the power and authority of the king was closely tied to his sacred function as the intermediary between the secular and the divine. Phoenician monarchs therefore created a symbiotic relationship with religion in order to establish divine legitimacy for their rule and thus ensure the support of the people. A number of Phoenician literary texts and inscriptions reveal that one of the king's primary roles was that of chief priest or religious functionary. Ethbaal (*c.* 915-847 BC), who was king of Tyre in the ninth century, is described by Josephus as a priest of Astarte. The same title was also taken by Eshmunazar and Tabnith, who were kings of Sidon during the fifth century, while king Ethbaal of Sidon (*c.* 940-908 BC) was still using the title 'priest of the Lady' as late as the fourth. In Tyre, the priesthood is known to be headed by the monarch, indicating that the sacred nature of the king's position was perhaps more prominent than in other Phoenician cities. This may, in part, be due to the power and influence of Melqart, the city's patron deity. However, although other kings may have played a less prominent role in the religious life of the city, they still demonstrated their piety through the restoration or construction of new temples. In general, Phoenician monarchs only functioned as chief priests for their city's primary deity, a situation that arose for two reasons: first, because it helped to confirm which god was pre-eminent among the city's pantheon; secondly, because it provided monarchs with a way of legitimising their rule as they could claim to be ruling under the auspices of a divine patron. If it is accepted that one of the main functions of a Phoenician sovereign was that of chief priest, it is logical to assume that they would have undertaken a number of religious duties, such as public sacrifices and the examination of entrails during important religious festivals. On occasion, Phoenician kings can be identified as going one step further and claiming divinity for themselves. For instance, the king of Tyre was harshly criticised by the Hebrew prophet Ezekiel for 'being swollen with pride, you have said: I am god. I am sitting on the throne of God, surrounded by seas'. Ezekiel continues, 'you are a man and not a god': here the prophet's obvious ire seems to indicate that the king of Tyre had been claiming divine status. The link between monarchy and divinity was made more explicit by the incorporation of divine names, such as Baal, Eshmun, Melqart and Astarte, into the king's dynastic or family name; for instance, the names of Hiram's sons, Abdastratus ('Servant of Astarte') and Baalbazer ('Servant of Baal'), illustrate this practice.

The Council of Elders

Confusion concerning the powers and prerogatives of the Phoenician monarchs has been generated because a number of ancient sources refer to a 'council of elders' or a 'merchant aristocracy'. In political and commercial matters, the kings of Tyre and Byblos seem to have been advised by a council of elders or representatives from the most respected and powerful families in the city. The Amarna Letters indicate that this system dates back at least as far as the middle of the second millennium

BC. In his letter to the Pharaoh, king Ribhaddi of Byblos mentions a group endowed with great power and importance within his city. This group seems to have operated as some kind of advisory council to the king and thus needed to be consulted before any decision could be made. Later accounts allude to this group as a governing body which acted alongside the king; its members were given the title 'Lords of the City'. In Tyre there was a similar council referred to by the Hebrew prophets, Isaiah and Ezekiel, as 'Princes of Tyre'. These men were also referred to as 'Princes of the Sea', giving rise to the suggestion that they formed part of a merchant oligarchy within the city. In the report of Wen-Amon, the king of Byblos, Zakarbaal, seeks the advice of his 'Council of State' when considering the demand by Tjekker that Wen-Amon should be handed over to him for punishment. Furthermore, an inscription from Sarepta also suggests the existence of a council or committee of ten who were responsible for helping to govern the city and its territory. A more explicit reference to a council of elders can be found in the treaty between the Assyrian king Esarhadon and king Baal of Tyre, dated to the middle of the seventh century. In this treaty, Esarhadon nominates an Assyrian governor who is to serve in Baal's 'court' and assist in the governing of the city. Moreover, Arrian, writing in the first century AD, documents that the king of Tyre dispatched his ambassadors to meet with Alexander the Great and negotiate on behalf of the city of Tyre: this may well refer to an assembly of citizens endowed with deliberative powers. Although we do not know how these councils of elders operated or what their political responsibilities were, the evidence suggests that they were prestigious committees that advised the king on important matters of state. Frustratingly, it is impossible to determine whether their role was purely consultative or formed a direct part of governmental decision making, but what is clear is that these councils were comprised of nobles and high ranking officials who could be relied upon to assist the king in resolving judicial, fiscal and religious matters. The inscription on the tomb of king Ahiram of Byblos records that the upper echelons of the city's social and political hierarchies consisted of the king, various councils and governors, and, finally, the commanders of the army. In addition to the council of elders, a number of ancient texts also refer to a larger citizen group known as the 'Peoples' Assembly'. This group's existence is documented in both Tyre and Sidon, and seems to have been composed of all free adult male citizens. As with the Council of Elders little is known about the nature, function and authority of this body, but scholarly opinion is that it simply affirmed decisions made by the king.

Social structure

It is a difficult task to try and identify the social structure of the Phoenician city-states. Although comparisons can be drawn with other Near Eastern societies these must be made tentatively. One certainty is that the populations of Phoenicia were socially stratified. A stratified society is one in which members of the same sex, and of equivalent age, do not have access to the same basic resources that sustain life. The three distinguishing features of a stratified society are: the exclusion of at least one segment of society, the tendency of high-ranking officials to socialise only with one another, and a social elite which ensures that some form of economic advantage accompanies their status. Although it is difficult to gauge the divide between wealthy and poor, the archaeological record suggests that the gap may have been considerable. Excavations of a number of Phoenician cemeteries have revealed a vast difference between the burial practices of the poor and those of the wealthy. The stark contrast in the quality of funerary monuments afforded by different social classes is also reflected in the housing sector. This suggests that the economic divide between rich and poor was considerable. A plausible reconstruction of the social hierarchy of a Phoenician city state would be:

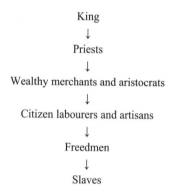

King
↓
Priests
↓
Wealthy merchants and aristocrats
↓
Citizen labourers and artisans
↓
Freedmen
↓
Slaves

Fig. 9. Phoenicia's social hierarchy.

Although a schematic overview of Phoenicia's social hierarchy can be generated, the lack of contemporary source material prevents more detailed analysis. Thus, for instance, it is impossible to identify the precise status attributed to individual occupations or to rank against each other the mass of individuals who comprised the so-called 'middle class'. Despite a considerable divide between rich and poor, with the vast majority of a city's wealth being controlled by the king, various priesthoods and the aristocracy, there is little evidence for political strife between the various social classes.

When considering the social makeup of the various Phoenician city-states it is also worth noting that, due to their commercial focus, they contained a highly transient and mobile population which included not only those whose profession relied on travel (such as merchants, hauliers, sailors and prospectors), but also those who by choice or by necessity worked abroad (including foreign artisans, craftsmen, miners, scribes and envoys). A Phoenician city would also have included a considerable number of transient foreigners (such as seasonal workers, traders and hauliers, slaves and official envoys), some of whom would have taken up temporary residence. This situation had two consequences: first, it encouraged social interaction between different socio-ethnic groups resulting in intermarriage between citizens and foreigners; secondly, it meant that most Phoenician city-states were home to a sizeable immigrant community. The overall picture which emerges is one of an ethnically mixed society that was willing to embrace rather than exclude foreigners and foreign culture.

Women

Although they were never considered legally equal to men, the relatively high status afforded to women in the Phoenician city-states (and in the ancient Near East in general) was due to the importance of goddesses within the religious pantheons. Women could therefore undertake various temple jobs, such as priestesses, musicians or singers. Moreover, the large temple complexes were staffed by managers, officials, scribes and labourers, and it is thought that some of the administrative positions in the temples would have been held by women. Those fortunate enough to hold such positions would have been from an aristocratic background, or perhaps even members of the royal family. Those women who were employed full time by the temple lived in cloisters and were forbidden to marry. Orphans and illegitimate children, both male and female, who ended up working in temples sometimes served as temple prostitutes, a function described in graphic detail by Herodotus. As was the case elsewhere in the Near East, Phoenician women contributed significantly to the local economy. Many cottage industries, such as weaving and textile manufacture, relied solely on the contribution of women. A funerary inscription from the Carthaginian *tophet* (places set aside for child burial and/or sacrifice), provides evidence which suggests that women could gain professional status and grow wealthy in their own right. The inscription records that the deceased, a Carthaginian woman named Shiboulet, had been a 'city-merchant', a fact which would seem to indicate that women could play an active role in Carthage's economy. This is not a unique situation, as the Ugaritic texts also reveal that women could, with their husbands' permission, take charge of a small business. However, despite having some limited role in the commercial life of a city, a woman's primary responsibility was to bear children, particularly sons. This was such an important aspect of women's lives that those who bore no children could be considered cursed. As with their contemporaries in Babylon, Assyria and Carthage, Phoenician women were able to inherit and bequeath property. Their legal rights, in particular those relating to property, must have been enshrined in written legal codes (like those discovered in Babylon, Assyria and Ugarit), but unfortunately none have survived.

Slaves and freedmen
Although few of the surviving literary texts shed much light on the lives of slaves, by combining the archaeological evidence with documents from other contemporary cultures such as Assyria, Babylon and later Carthage, it is possible partially to reconstruct the lives of Phoenician slaves. For example, the Carthaginian author, Mago, bears testimony to the widespread use of slaves as part of the Punic workforce and, from this evidence, historians have extrapolated that slaves similarly composed a large percentage of the labour force in Phoenicia proper. In an agricultural context, slaves were widely employed as field hands, working in conjunction with semi-dependent rural workers. In the urban sphere, slaves were employed in a variety of capacities including as artisans, craftsmen, manual labourers, industrial workers, and servants on large estates. No doubt some of those employed as estate workers would have functioned as clerks, scribes, administrators and even managers. Although it is likely that there were social distinctions made between different types of slaves (i.e. captives, prisoners of war, convicts or chattel slaves), such distinctions are impossible to recover. Household slaves, as in other Near Eastern cultures, tended to be female although, on rare occasions, male slaves could also reside with a family. Slave owners encouraged their slaves to marry in order to increase their wealth, as offspring from such unions belonged to the master. Even though the master was free to sell these children it was rare for members of the same family to be separated. A male slave could, with his master's consent, marry a free woman: even if this woman brought no dowry with her, she, and her children, remained free. All slave-girls were eligible to be considered concubines, whether they were specifically supplied by a barren wife who wished to use them

as a surrogate mother, or were simply owned by the husband as part of his household staff. If, as a concubine, the slave bore her owner no children, she remained in servitude and could be sold at any time. In contrast, a concubine who did bear children would remain with the family and could expect manumission upon the death of her master, as could her children.

Another social class that is well attested in Carthage, and which must also have been present in the cities of Phoenicia, was that of 'freedman'. Freedmen were former slaves who had been allowed to purchase or earn their manumission. In fact, Mago actively encouraged masters to allow their slaves to earn their freedom; not for any humanitarian reason, but so that the slaves would be content and thus more likely to work harder. The class of freedman must have been a significant one; evidence from Carthage shows that the state not only condoned the freeing of slaves but actually institutionalised it. A Punic legal decree dating to the fourth century documents that the formal freeing of slaves actually required the permission of the citizen assembly.

Phoenician cities
In Lebanon, archaeological investigation has been hindered by the fact that a number of the major settlements lie underneath modern buildings; consequently, it is extremely difficult to identify evidence of coherent attempts at town planning. The following sections, therefore, merely try to identify the main features of Phoenician architecture rather than discuss the unique urban development of individual sites. In comparison with other cities within the continental Near East, in particular those of Syria, Egypt and Mesopotamia, the Phoenician cities were relatively small in size. Smallish towns, such as Beirut and Sarepta, were between c. 2-6 hectares; larger cities, such as Arwad, Byblos and Sidon, could reach in excess of 40 hectares. Of the mainland cities, Arwad (c. 40 hectares) and Sidon (c. 60 hectares) were the largest, while, in contrast to its importance, Tyre was only a medium-sized city, reaching a maximum area of 16 hectares.

The archaeological evidence pertaining to Phoenician city-planning and architecture allows the identification of certain constant features that combine to delineate a specifically Phoenician type of settlement. One of the most obvious was the choice of topographical location: where possible, Phoenician cities and colonies were sited on promontories, or on islets not far from the coast. These locations not only provided easy access to the sea and all its associated resources, they also provided defensive advantages, as cities on islets or promontories were difficult to storm or

Fig. 10. Iron Age city walls at the Israelite settlement of Tel Dan
(author's photo).

blockade. In general, the majority of Phoenician cities, whether walled
citadels, colonies or trading emporia, have shown a remarkably similar
layout, suggesting that some form of proto-city planning was in operation.
At the heart of each settlement was a walled citadel around which other
districts were established, including residential areas, religious centres,
and commercial and industrial zones. The typical Phoenician settlement
was composed of two distinct districts: 'a lower town', which housed the
business and residential regions, and an 'upper city', which accommo-
dated the major temples, administrative buildings, and residences of the
wealthy. The upper district also formed a defensive citadel which could
be isolated from the rest of the city during times of siege. The whole city
was often encompassed by a series of curtain walls designed to divide the
city into separate defensible zones. Located outside the city walls were
cemeteries and *tophets*. The commercial life of the Phoenician city was
unsurprisingly organised around the port facilities, markets and ware-
houses. The primary focus was the city's *emporium* (large market place)
which was situated in a location accessible from both the harbour and the
city's main gate. Heavy industrial activity, including metal-working,
dyeing and tanning, was kept separate from the residential regions of the
'lower district'. The reason for this was twofold: first, there were health

considerations (for instance the risk of fires or disease); secondly, there was the awful smell that accompanied these activities. If possible, these industries were located near the harbour, a solution that had the practical advantage of enabling commodities destined for export to be quickly shipped. Smaller cottage industries, such as textile weaving, faience manufacture and pottery production, were typically spread throughout the city and not centred in or around one particular location.

Construction methods and materials
The climate and readily available natural resources determined building styles and construction techniques in ancient Phoenicia. These factors not only influenced the appearance of buildings and how they were decorated but also their survival in the archaeological record. Mud-and-wattle was one of the first and most widely used techniques for building houses. The building process began with a simple wooden frame, made from long, thin poles or reeds. Mesopotamian builders often used a plant known as the 'Giant Reed' which could grow to over 6 m tall to construct their frames. The reeds and poles were woven together to produce a strong exoskeleton or wattle work. This wattle work was then plastered with mud or clay which would harden naturally in the sun. Mud-and-wattle constructions could survive for many years in regions with a low average rainfall; moreover, they were easy to maintain and repair. The houses would have a corbelled dome roof made from woven reeds, or, later, mud bricks. The next major advance in structural engineering was the construction of mud-brick buildings. Phoenicia had access to plenty of clay and mud which lined the banks of the rivers that criss-crossed the region. The earliest use of mud in construction involved building solid walls from packed mud and clay. The result was crude, uneven walls of varying thickness, which were prone to crumble and collapse. In order to combat such problems the next technological advancement was the creation of mud bricks (see Fig. 11). Mud and/or clay was packed into four-sided wooden frames and left to dry in the sun; once hardened, the bricks could be used to construct straight, uniform walls. Eventually, builders realised that by mixing chopped straw with the mud or clay, they could produce stronger bricks that were less likely to crack during the hardening process. Phoenician builders also made use of bitumen as a sealant against damp and water.

Aside from mud bricks, Phoenician builders were heavily reliant on timber. Good building timber was plentiful in the Levant and a range of different trees were used in construction. For general purposes, such as fittings and frames, the Phoenicians used sycamore fig, Aleppo pine and

Fig. 11. Mud-brick walls and arched gateway at the Canaanite/Phoenician city of Laish, constructed *c*. 1750 BC (author's photo).

oak (*terebinth*), while for roofing planks and structural timbers, they utilised cypress, poplar, pine and oak. Phoenician cedars were the most prized wood for magnificent building projects as they were immensely strong but not brittle. By *c*. 7000 BC it was already understood by Phoenician builders that masonry walls, whether of mud-brick or stone construction, were solid enough to bear the load of an entire structure: accordingly there was a move away from the corbelled mud-brick dome roof towards a flat mud roof set over timber beams. The most salient changes in building materials and techniques were occasioned by the need for massive urban fortifications. Solid walls sufficiently tall to inhibit escalade, and with a total length of several km, had to be thrown up quickly (see Fig. 10). The basic building materials for these walls were rubble stone and mud brick. However, since there was no basic change in the quality of masonry, an enormous quantitative change was needed to achieve the required height; consequently, some city walls were between 5 and 10 m deep. The bonding pattern of the bricks used in these walls continued to be the simple stretcher-bond style (a pattern made by laying bricks, with their length in the direction of the face of the wall, one on top of another, while ensuring that each vertical brick is positioned between the centres of the brick above and below).

At the same time as the construction of these walls, it is also possible to see the development of new designs for public buildings. For example, both palaces and sanctuaries demanded a larger, open-unit plan which necessitated the development of pillar, post or column construction. Although traditionally pillars and columns had been used only for doubling and reinforcing walls, they were now utilised to construct large columnar porticos and halls. At Byblos, probably as a result of its proximity to a ready supply of cedar wood, prototype hypostyle halls (i.e. halls that have roofs or ceilings supported by rows of columns) appear early in the Bronze Age. Over time, columns came to be used fairly generally in palaces and temples; however, the Phoenicians never developed their own columnar style but instead occasionally adopted different column types from neighbouring cultures (Greece and Egypt). Despite not developing a unique columnar style, the Phoenicians did develop a pilaster capital which they exported to Cyprus. This was the prototype Aeolic capital used to dignify ceremonial portals by way of engaged piers and jambs. Moreover, contrary to the popular belief that the Romans invented arches and domes, Mesopotamian builders were using these architectural features as early as the middle Bronze Age.

During the mid to late Bronze Age, elements of monumental stone building appear for the first time in the Levant. Although sandstone and basalt were used on occasion, the region's main building stone was generally limestone. At first the use of shaped stone was confined to isolated blocks, but during the late Bronze Age finely dressed blocks were used for more extended passages (see Fig. 12). With the increasing resources of the Phoenician city-states, fine stone masonry became a notable feature of buildings in Phoenicia. However, this monumental masonry belonged to a very distinctive style of stone dressing. It presented the appearance of finely jointed ashlar (a squared block of building stone) on the face of the stone; however, all the joints opened widely to the interior so that in reality it was ashlar-faced coarse rubble. This type of stonework was neither in the style of Pharaonic Egypt nor of later Greek masonry, and seems to have been confined to the Levant. Since there is no evidence in Phoenicia for lifting devices such as hoists, winches and pulley blocks, lifting lugs or lewis holes, archaeologists have proposed that all heavy construction relied on the same method. This was the method of monumental masonry used in Egypt. It was highly labour intensive and so was not for everyday application. Instead, it would appear that massive units were, as a rule, kept close to ground level while the superstructure was raised and set in place by workman operating with ladders, planks and ropes.

Fig. 12. Late Bronze Age ashlar-faced walls at the Canaanite city of Megiddo (author's photo).

Housing

During much of the Bronze Age, the building of houses was a family affair whereas the first specialised master builders probably directed and supervised the raising of city walls. Therefore, prior to the late Bronze Age there is little evidence of architectural planning or co-ordination; instead, each dwelling seems to have had its own unique design. However, by the late Bronze Age to early Iron Age, there seems to be some standardisation of size and design. Continuing excavations at sites in southern Phoenicia and Carthage are helping to provide new insights into Phoenician domestic architecture. These excavations have shown that a typical Phoenician house, dating to the early Iron Age, comprised three or four moderately sized rooms arranged in varying configurations. Frequently, a large open hallway provided access to two or three smaller, adjacent rooms at the rear of the premises. Similar three- or four-room dwellings were also popular throughout the Levant and thus our knowledge of Phoenician domestic architecture has been supplemented through studying the construction techniques and structural designs found in contemporary cultures. Due to the compact dimensions of the average Phoenician town, the residential district of each city tended to be crowded with each private dwelling fighting for space. With free space at a premium, many houses solved the problem by expanding upwards rather than outwards: as a rule the average Phoenician house had at least two storeys. When present, upper floors replicated the plan of the ground floor and were constructed on extra thick walls which provided the necessary support and stability. Strabo documents that the houses at Tyre and Arwad had more than two storeys, even claiming that the Tyrian high-rises were taller than those found in Rome. Frescos and paintings have also provided evidence for the appearance of Phoenician houses. Comparisons of Phoenician houses found on the reliefs in Sennacherib's palace with those found in the cruder tomb paintings discovered at Djebel, a Phoenician colony in North Africa, has revealed a 'typical' style of Phoenician dwelling. The tomb painting shows a town with battlements and walls, within which are 17 two-storey houses of differing sizes. If one compares this representation with those found on the reliefs carved for Sennacherib, it is possible to identify a remarkable similarity between the architecture they portray. The Sennacherib relief, which has as its subject the sacking of a Phoenician town, also depicts houses that are two stories, suggesting that this was typical. This is a hypothesis backed up by the archaeological excavations at Horvat Rosh Zayit in Lower Galilee, which have revealed an early fortified Phoenician residence. The ground plan of the house consists of a central hall surrounded by eight variously sized rooms that seem to have served as offices or commercial storage facilities. The complex was found to have originally had two floors with the level of the upper floor being identifiable by the survival of stone thresholds; this upper floor is believed to have housed the living quarters. The entire complex was enclosed by a massive wall with four corner towers. The structure, which dates to the period spanning the mid-tenth to mid-ninth centuries BC, offers a rare insight into the domestic style of architecture afforded by the elite.

Additionally, recent excavations on the Byrsa hill at Carthage have uncovered a Phoenician residence which is so well-preserved that it has been possible for archaeologists to trace its evolution through a 200-year period – from the eighth to the sixth century BC. In its second construction phase, the house was a long rectangular building which consisted of a large enclosed courtyard behind which were a series of four rooms arranged in longitudinal pairs. In its general characteristics and construction (i.e. mud brick built on a stone foundation), the dwelling is reminiscent of late Bronze Age houses of the northern Levant. Since Carthage was a colony of Tyre, the house in all probability represents the type of urban dwelling found in the Phoenician mother-city. In its third building phase, the interior of the house was reconfigured as a courtyard-less, four-room residence with three long parallel chambers at the front and a large room (spanning the building's width) at the back. The origins of this style of house can also be traced back to the Phoenician mainland, and again serve to highlight the close cultural links between mother-city and colony. In the second half of the seventh century BC, the house was once again remodelled and now utilised a new wall construction technique known as 'opus Africanum'. This involved alternating zones of mud brick and rubble, with monolithic piers designed to strengthen the wall. In essence this 'new' technique was a variant on the pier-and-rubble technique utilised by the Phoenician engineers of the mainland. The main difference between the mainland and Punic techniques was the manner in which the upright piers were constructed; in Phoenicia proper they were monolithic carved blocks, while in Carthage they were built up from individual ashlar blocks stacked in a 'header' and 'stretcher' fashion. As for the superstructure, the house appears to have been two-storeyed, with access to the upper floor provided by an inner staircase located at the rear of the dwelling. The second floor appears to have been supported by internal pillars and spanned by wooden beams; a style reminiscent of those found at sites throughout the Levant.

Water supplies and drainage
In general, the fresh water supply of most cities was procured from local sources, such as rivers and springs. For the most part large cities were built in regions known to have sufficient access to plentiful supplies of fresh water. However, when local supplies proved to be inadequate, a situation regularly faced by Tyre, water had to be piped in or physically imported in large ceramic jars. When necessary, existing water supplies could be supplemented by excavated wells, or by constructing lime plastered cisterns designed to capture rain water. Small cisterns would often be constructed on the roofs of Phoenician houses, giving each dwelling its own independent water supply. This practice was prevalent in Carthage and seems to have been a concept exported from Tyre where a number of similar cisterns have been discovered. In Carthage, nearly all courtyards were marked by the presence of an excavated well or an impluvium for the collection of rainwater: once collected this water would then be stored in an underground cistern. The lining of cisterns with impermeable lime-based plaster was an important technological development as it made it possible to store rainwater for longer periods. Consequently, settlers were no longer obliged to found their colonies near to springs or streams. The importation of cement mixing techniques from Greece was another great advance in the storage of water as it enabled the

construction of larger, less permeable cisterns. However, the greatest scientific marvel for capturing fresh water was the system developed by the citizens of Arwad. Having founded their city on a large, solid rock face, the Arwadians found they were unable to drill wells or tap into underground supplies of fresh water; as a result, they were forced to look for alternative sources. Strabo records that in order to overcome the problem, the engineers of Arwad developed a method for collecting the fresh water which constantly gushed out of the sea-bed close to the city. From their boats, the engineers carefully positioned down-turned lead funnels over the geysers; this increased the pressure and forced the freshwater closer to the surface where it could be collected in leather pipes. This was such an effective system that in Greece fresh water was still being collected in this manner until the late 1970s.

In addition to cisterns, many Phoenician houses were also equipped with basic stone channel gutters. Recent excavations in the small North African town of Dar Essafi, which have unearthed a number of houses dating to the late third or early second century, show that even in this relative backwater the settlement was still found to have a complex and well-developed drainage system. One of the more affluent houses contained a small bathroom which included a well-preserved bath and toilet, both of which were connected to a carefully planned drainage system. This drainage system consisted of clay pipes which carried waste water to a main sewer constructed of baked mud bricks. Although archaeologists have yet to uncover the drainage system of a mainland Phoenician city, it is likely that they would be similar to those excavated at Dar Essafi and Carthage. It is worth noting, however, that although some of the more affluent citizens had baths within their homes, toilets were generally located in separate public facilities. Furthermore, archaeology has shown that the homes of ordinary workers and peasants had neither communal bathroom nor lavatories. Instead, the poor, if they did not live near to public latrines, would defecate outside in orchards, in fields, or even in the street. In Phoenicia, having human waste outdoors was not necessarily a health risk since the hot sun dried and sterilised faecal matter within hours. Rubbish was normally deposited in the streets or on vacant plots of land and the discovery of small layers of ash suggests that these heaps might regularly have been burnt; however, there was no formal municipal rubbish collection or disposal. The prevalence of animal teeth and bones at Phoenician sites suggest that there were large numbers of stray dogs and pigs that would scavenge throughout the city. Rodents also thrived and presented a constant threat to the health of the population as they transmitted disease and fleas.

Harbours

A central feature of every Phoenician settlement was its harbours, which formed the commercial heartland of the city. This is unsurprising given that the Phoenicians relied heavily on maritime trade and communication. Unfortunately, documentation for Phoenician ports prior to the Hellenistic and Roman periods is virtually non-existent. In terms of configuration, Phoenician harbours were either 'open' or 'closed', depending upon the width of the harbour mouth and how easily it could be defended. An open harbour was one which was unsheltered and exposed to the sea, while a closed harbour was one that was naturally, or artificially, sheltered from the sea and had a narrow entrance that was easily defensible. Literary evidence suggests that an open harbour could be closed off during times of war by the use of a chain. Before the fourth to third centuries BC, the technique of building walls and laying foundations underwater had yet to be discovered. Consequently, scholars avoid using terms such as 'wharves' or 'harbour complexes' until their formal appearance in the Hellenistic period. Studies of ancient Phoenician ports have shown that prior to the fourth century, the conditions of a site were naturally exploited to form harbours, either by carving out the natural rock or adapting reefs or rocky islands to form moles or breakwaters. Natural reefs were frequently supplemented by the construction of walls on top of them, this produced sheltered harbours or lagoons that could be several km wide. In the absence of proper harbour facilities, vessels could simply be dragged up onto the beach. The city of Tyre was serviced by two ports, one to the south of the city that was artificially carved out of the rock, and the second, in the north, which was naturally protected by a series of reefs. A great many Phoenician cities emulated Tyre's model in order to take advantage of twin harbour complexes. For instance, the open or external harbour could be used for foreign merchant vessels, while the closed, or inner harbour, would be intended for local traffic and military vessels. It seems that this was the case at Arwad, Sidon and Tell Sukas, among others. The city of Atlit on Israel's northern coast offers the earliest and most complete example of an Iron Age Phoenician harbour complex. The port reveals the Phoenicians' technical sophistication in methods of harbour construction, and, in particular their ability to construct vertical ashlar walls underwater with a precision which eliminated the need for mortar or clamps. In order to construct a firm foundation for these underwater walls, either the bedrock was levelled or a thin layer of loose pebbles was poured in, in order to fill any large gaps or cracks in the ocean floor. The superstructure of the wall consisted of finely cut ashlar stones that were laid as 'headers' (i.e. laid at a right angle to the face of a wall so that only their short ends showed). By laying them in this manner, Phoenician engineers ensured that their wall provided maximum resistance to the destructive motion of the waves. In order to avoid silting and the build up of marine debris, a second, narrower sea exit was constructed; this smaller opening essentially served as a flushing conduit for the harbour basin.

Chapter 5

The Economy

Literary and archaeological evidence combine to show that the original basis of the Phoenician economies was agriculture and husbandry. By 6000 BC, all the staple crops known from later texts were already being cultivated, the basic herd animals had been domesticated, and irrigation systems were being established. The availability of profitable and nutritious crops such as barley and wheat, in addition to the development of the plough and systems of irrigation, contributed to the emergence of flourishing agricultural economies. By 1200 BC, however, the majority of the Phoenician city-states also had burgeoning maritime economies. By situating their cities close to the sea, the Phoenicians were able to procure and transport large quantities of raw material easily and efficiently. Moreover, the sea was an integral component of three of Phoenicia's main industries, namely fishing, purple dye production and shipbuilding. Finally, the sea facilitated commerce, enabling the Phoenicians to establish wide-reaching trade networks that linked Egypt, the Aegean and Western Europe. As with so many aspects of Phoenician civilisation, we possess very little direct evidence concerning the various commercial infrastructures: therefore, while the sources may tell us a great deal about Phoenician trade networks and commercial ties with foreign states, they provide little information about the primary mechanisms of economic control or the institutions that administered them. What is clear, however, is that by the twelfth century the Phoenician economies had become 'mixed economies' (i.e. they incorporated prominent agricultural, industrial and commercial sectors).

Agriculture

Although there is little direct evidence pertaining to Phoenician agricultural systems and techniques, it is possible to piece together a plausible reconstruction of Phoenician agrarian operations by examining the farming techniques used in contemporary societies, such as Assyria, Israel, and Babylon, and by considering the 40 fragments of the Carthaginian author Mago who wrote a detailed treatise on Punic agricultural practices.

In general agricultural production was carried out by several sections of Phoenician society: first, the temple and palace farmed the extensive land under their control, either directly or through a system of leases; secondly, there were the wealthy and moderately affluent farmers who owned land holdings of various sizes; thirdly, there were the city's poor nomads and shepherds who were allotted small plots of land to cultivate. The amount of land held by each of these groups, and the volume of crops they produced, cannot be established definitively and probably varied according to the time period, region and condition of the soil. In general, the most fertile territories were used to support temples and the household administrations of the monarchy and high-ranking state officials. Minor and middle-ranking officials held relatively small plots of land which were worked by others but which ensured a comfortable living. By comparison, the small-scale, private farmer – these made up a significant percentage of the agrarian population – probably drove the plough himself, only utilising seasonal labourers to help speed up ploughing or harvesting when absolutely necessary. The costs of farming were high and included seed, plough, tools and draft animals (which were expensive to keep as oxen needed plenty of food in order to undertake sustained labour). The labourers also needed to be fed, either in rations or by a residual share of the crops. Consequently, many poorer farmers kept small numbers of poultry that could be used to help supplement the farm's income. Moreover, the manufacture of textiles by female family members was another common method for increasing a farm's modest income. The efficient management of a farm was therefore based on skilfully combining a variety of rural occupations at different times in the agricultural cycle.

Cereal crops and vegetables
The largest component of the domestic economy was agriculture and husbandry. There is no doubt that the Phoenicians exploited the small amount of fertile land to the greatest extent possible. Archaeological investigation has revealed that the Phoenicians cultivated the lower slopes of the Lebanese mountains, thereby making use of all available sources of water and arable land. With many parts of Phoenicia experiencing frequent water shortages and because of the salinity of the soil, the Phoenicians turned to irrigation to ensure healthy crop yields. The majority of streams suitable for irrigation were located on the coastal plains: accordingly, these regions formed the agricultural hinterland of the various city-states. Cities such as Tyre, which had a high density of population, also succeeded in irrigating their land and providing drinking water

for their citizens through the development of complex drainage networks and the construction of large cisterns. Water was brought to the fields by the use of branch canals and feeder channels which ran along the top of artificial dikes. Other Near Eastern cultures utilised weirs to raise the water level in the larger streams, and it is highly probable that the Phoenicians employed similar systems. These methods of irrigations enabled the intensive cultivation of crops, a situation referred to by Ezekiel when comparing the Phoenician coastal plain with the Garden of Eden. Even so, Phoenicia had a grain deficit. The cereal crops which were grown on the mountain sides could not meet the needs of a population that had been expanding constantly from the middle of the Iron Age. Consequently, any terrain that could be properly irrigated was used to grow cereal crops, while the rockier soil was used for plantations or to graze herds. Within Phoenicia itself the extensive cultivation of grain was only possible in the northerly Akkar plain and in the fertile Beqa valley to the south. Once harvested the grain was stored in large silos which were designed to protect and preserve it. Barley was able to withstand salinity and aridity better than wheat and thus became a staple of the Phoenician diet. Barley was also used as a means of exchange, with an accepted value just like silver or gold and so wages were often paid in barley quotas. The region's narrow alluvial coastal plain clearly limited the potential for agricultural development, especially the cultivation of cereal crops. Therefore, in addition to barley and wheat, the Phoenicians also grew vegetables and fruit including onions, garlic, leeks, turnips, lettuces, cucumbers, apples and pomegranates. Vegetables and fruit needed more careful attention than barley and wheat and thus these were often cultivated separately on small plots.

Viticulture
Of the alternative sources of food available to the Phoenicians, the most important were grapes, olives, figs and dates. The country's soil and climate were ideally suited for viticulture. Therefore, by the end of the fifth century, Phoenicia had gained a reputation for producing the finest olives and grapes. This reputation for quality meant that Phoenician fruits were exported throughout the Mediterranean both in their raw and processed forms (i.e. as wine or olive oil). Olive trees and vines which need several years to start producing fruit but are productive for many seasons are indicators of economic and political stability and have a threefold importance: first, they were grown with limited rainfall and on relatively poor ground; secondly, they were harvested at different times of year to cereal crops meaning that manpower could be productively exploited

throughout the year; thirdly, they provided storable crops – olives as oil, and grapes as dried raisins or fermented wine – that could be used to supplement the daily diet or which provided some insurance against crops failure. Olive oil was particularly valuable as it could be used widely in food preparation, as a perfumed ointment for bathing, and as lamp fuel. Owing to its use as a fuel, olive oil was a necessary expense for most families and thus became a highly profitable industry. The discovery, in a number of Phoenician cities, towns and villages, of large stones with holes in the centre, used for crushing olives and grapes, attests to the widespread production of oil and wine. Since the production of wine and olive oil involved the use of expensive equipment, it is likely that communities shared these tools and produced wine or olive oil collectively. The Phoenicians are known to have been avid wine drinkers and it formed an integral part of their staple diet. Even the icons of Phoenician philosophy, Zeno of Citium and Chrysippus of Soli, are recorded as being 'serious wine drinkers'. In fact Zeno was so fond of wine that he is said to have died as the result of drinking too much. Phoenician wine would have been very sweet, and although the grapes were fermented, the alcohol level was quite low. When drunk the wine would have been diluted with water (possibly in a ratio of 50% water 50% wine), and it was only during religious festivals, or when undertaking religious rituals, that wine would be consumed neat. Scholars have argued that this may account for why intoxication was considered as akin to a spiritual state in a number of Near Eastern religions. As wine and oil were both part of the staple diet they were also a major source of income for Phoenician farmers. The discovery of Phoenician transport amphorae attests to the extensive export market for these products. In 1999, archaeologists discovered the remains of two Phoenician merchant vessels which had been transporting wine. The team recovered a number of intact amphorae that had been perfectly preserved due to bitterly cold temperatures, a lack of direct sunlight, and the intense pressure of the water. The containers were found to have been sealed with a plug that took the form of a pinewood disk embedded into the neck of the amphorae using a clay and resin mix. This formed an air-tight seal that preserved the contents and prevented spillage while in transit. A careful investigation of these containers has demonstrated that Phoenician amphorae were produced in standardised capacities specifically to facilitate the export of oil and wine.

Livestock

The type of livestock most prevalent in Phoenicia was cattle; however, the Phoenicians also reared considerable numbers of asses (for their carrying capacity), sheep (for their wool) and goats (primarily for milk). As these animals were chiefly reared for their produce, they were rarely eaten as a source of meat. Sheep and goats, which were among the first animals to be domesticated, were known as 'small cattle' and were kept in large flocks that belonged to the state, the temple or private owners. The foothills of the Lebanese mountains provided ample pasture for sizeable flocks, watched over by hired hands. These pastoralists would spend only a small portion of the year with the community and were responsible for protecting the herds from predators such as lions and wolves. If an animal was killed by a predator the shepherd had to present the remains of the carcass to the owner in order to prove that the animal had not been stolen by the watchmen. If a death occurred as a result of negligence by the herder, then he would have to compensate the owner. Shepherds would also be responsible for herding the flocks to various pastures dotted around the landscape. Modern-day Bedouin still practise pastoralism in the same way as their ancient ancestors: they spend the wetter months camped on the fringes of the desert, and once the vegetation had been consumed by grazing or withered by the summer heat they move their flocks to less extreme environments, such as the foothills of the mountains. This system ensures that they make the most of the limited resources at their disposal. In addition to sheep and goats, cows were also prevalent in Phoenicia and were important as they produced milk which could be used to make butter, yoghurt, cheese and ghee. Oxen, on the other hand, were valuable as they could be used to draw seeder-ploughs which prepared the land for sowing. A Punic stele illustrating this type of plough closely resembles the one described by Mago in his treatise on Carthaginian agriculture. Another beast of burden was the ass which could be used to pull ploughs and carts; caravans of wild donkeys were also used by Phoenician merchants to transport commodities into the interior of Asia Minor. Although the Phoenicians bred horses, they were expensive to feed and thus rarely used as draught animals: instead they were primarily employed by the elite for hunting or for warfare.

Domestic animals

The dog was one of the earliest domesticated animals and was principally used to protect herds and dwellings against predators. To date archaeologists have been able to distinguish only two breeds of dog: large greyhounds which were mainly used for hunting, and a very strong breed (in the order of danes and mastiffs) which was suitable for herding and for use as an attack dog. Another important category of domestic animal was poultry, such as chickens, geese and ducks, which were prized as a source of meat but also for their eggs. The chicken was first reared in the Near East during the first millennium BC, subsequently arriving in Greece during the late seventh or early sixth century. Geese were first raised in Babylon at the end of the third millennium BC, while the duck was introduced to the region early in the second millennium BC. Although all three were raised in significant numbers, chicken bones have been found in the largest quantities and seemed to have become a staple part of the diet during the Persian period. Beekeeping was another important agricultural industry. The so-called European honeybee (*Apis mellifera*) was found in the ancient Near East, and its existence is documented in central Iran, Anatolia, the Levant and Egypt. By the second millennium, honey and beeswax were used for a variety of purposes including as a medicine and as a waterproof sealant; honey was also the Phoenicians' primary source of sugar. The earliest evidence for hive beekeeping (apiculture) comes from Old Kingdom Egypt (third millennium BC), and is found in a tomb painting depicting the gathering, filtering and packing of honey. Typical pipe hives made of mud or clay are about a metre long and are stacked together. The ends are sealed except for small holes that allow the bees to pass in and out of the hive. There are no textual references to beekeeping in ancient Phoenicia prior to the Hellenistic period, but the Israelite name for the region, 'Canaan', can be understood as 'the land of milk and honey' which suggests that beekeeping was widespread within the region. Our understanding of apiculture in the ancient Levant is constantly changing: the recent discovery of beehives at Tel Rehove has shown that beekeeping in the Levant probably occurred as early as the tenth or ninth century BC.

Trade and commerce: the commercial sector

The Phoenicians, as we have seen, were traders first and foremost. Thus it is appropriate to examine the importance of inter-regional trade and the social and political institutions linked to it. This means exploring the role played by the state, the palace, the various religious institutions, and private companies in forging commercial ties and creating trade networks. The political systems of the late Bronze Age were based on large regional centres that were dominated by the palace. As a result, inter-state political and commercial relationships were between royal houses of equivalent rank. Merchants were under the influence of the palace and trading relations were dominated by the exchange of gifts (when dealing with a trade partner) and by tribute (when addressed to partners of lower rank). From the fourteenth century onwards commerce and diplomacy became intermingled. The trader, who was fully integrated into the public sector, not only took part in public administration but was entrusted by the state with organising commercial agencies and with buying and selling in his capacity of envoy of the king. In a number of respects, the palace-based economies of Phoenicia were similar to those of other contemporary societies such as Greece, Crete, Cyprus and Northern Syria. The late Bronze Age archives from Ugarit reveal the type of reciprocal trading ties that existed between influential commercial states. At Ugarit, Phoenician traders were part of commercial syndicates or trading partnerships, known as *huburs*. This institution appears in the Egyptian text *The Tale of Wen-Amon*, which informs us that a *hubur* involving 20 ships was jointly managed by the king of Byblos and the Egyptian pharaoh Smendes. The Old Testament records that the kings Hiram and Solomon entered into a similar partnership when they launched their trading expedition to Ophir. In Phoenicia, the *hubur* appears to have been an institution reserved for the head of state when creating inter-regional trading partnerships. Furthermore, reports, such as those by Wen-Amon, indicate that mercantile activity was strictly supervised by the king through the use of maritime officials such as the Harbour Master. The surviving evidence therefore suggests that prior to *c.* 1000 BC the king and palace seemed to have been the facilitator of most trade-related activities. It is not until the eighth century, when private commerce began to flourish, that a sizeable 'mercantile community' was to develop.

Phoenician merchants

In Phoenicia, as in the rest of the ancient Near East, traders enjoyed enormous social status and prestige, frequently sharing in the profit of the palace and occasionally forming part of the ruling family. The Phoenician trader was considered by his countrymen to be a qualified professional and specialist who devoted himself to business and to diplomacy. The *tamkaru* (wealthy merchants) were responsible for the face-to-face exchange of commodities (although occasionally they employed commercial representatives) and frequently operated as moneylenders, offering finance to their less wealthy peers. During the seventh and sixth centuries it is also possible to identify Phoenician merchants forming professional associations and family run 'houses' of merchants that were similar in form and function to medieval trade guilds; and so, private, or perhaps more accurately, independent merchants, operated within family units whose members inherited business from each other. This system ensured that there was loyalty between the various members of the company and that business interests were not damaged by infighting or factional disputes. Within this commercial infrastructure the royal house acted just like any other consortium or family operation. Monarchs involved themselves in commerce, not in order to fix prices or gain economic advantage for the state through treaties, but to make profit. So, in contrast to Greece, what we find in the Phoenician economy is a merging of public and private commercial interests. By the middle of the sixth century there seem to have been two distinct categories of merchant: those who operated on behalf of the royal house, and those who were part of a mercantile aristocracy. In a treaty signed between king Esarhadon of Assyria and king Baal of Tyre (c. 670 BC) this division is made explicit. The document distinctly refers to the 'ships of Baal' and the ships of 'the people of Tyre', on which sailing restrictions were imposed.

Pre-coinage economies
Prior to the adoption of coinage in the fifth century, the Phoenicians developed a series of regulated commercial agreements with their trade partners (in essence a barter economy). These treaties standardised the relative value of each type of raw material that was to be traded, and were especially useful when conducting business with one of the Great Powers (i.e. Egypt, Hatti, Babylon, Assyria or Mittani). This type of price fixing arrangement clearly underpinned Phoenician commerce from an early period and can be identified in *The Tale of Wen-Amon*. This document, written in the eleventh century BC, details the goods and raw materials that the Egyptian court provided to the Byblian royal house as payment for a large consignment of Phoenician cedar. The list of items dispatched by Pharaoh includes gold, silver, linen, papyrus rolls, cow-hides and rope. The relative value of each commodity used as payment was clearly based upon a predetermined exchange rate set against the accepted value of cedar wood. These trade agreements also seem to have fixed the equivalencies of goods for services. This was particularly important for the Phoenician cities as their service industries often comprised a sizeable part of their economy. An illustrative example of the profitability of Phoenician service industries can be identified in the financial agreement reached by the kings Solomon and Hiram of Tyre. Solomon sought the help of Hiram when constructing the new temple of Jerusalem, under the terms of agreement Hiram would not only provide raw materials (such as cedar and fir) but would also provide the services and expertise of his skilled woodcutters. These men would not only cut and transport the raw timber to the construction site, but would also prepare and shape the wood once it had been delivered. In return for these services, Solomon would provide the Tyrian king with a large annual contribution of agricultural products including wheat and oil. Semiramis, a mythical Assyrian queen,

is also reported to have made use of Phoenician shipwrights and craftsmen when building the riverboats she needed for her invasion of India. A further insight into early Phoenician barter economies is provided by Herodotus when he discusses the trade between Carthage and the Libyan tribes of North Africa. Herodotus claims that the Carthaginians, when trading with the Libyans living beyond the Pillars of Hercules, reintroduced a system of barter. Having left their goods on the beach the Carthaginian merchants would return to their ships and raise a smoke signal. The native Libyans would then evaluate the commodities and leave a pile of gold which they felt was commensurate, having done this, they would retire a suitable distance and wait for the Carthaginians' response. This coming and going continued until the Carthaginian merchants were happy with the price being offered and left. According to Herodotus, neither side broke the sanctity of this arrangement: the Carthaginians did not touch the gold until satisfied and the Libyans did not take the commodities until the Carthaginians had left. The Greek writer pseudo-Scylax also records a barter system when describing the trading relations between the Phoenicians and the Ethiopians. In this account, the Phoenicians are recorded as exchanging unguents, Egyptian stone (possibly meaning glass), and Attic vases for animal skins, elephant tusks and ivory. Again, there seems to have been a formal acceptance of the commensurability of each commodity.

Coinage

Although the use of coinage had become the norm in Greece by the early years of the sixth century, the Phoenicians did not adopt the practice of minting coins until far later. This situation is perhaps not unexpected due to the Phoenicians' willingness to interact with, and often exploit, less developed peoples. Therefore, with a long history of fixed exchange involving raw materials, metals and foodstuffs, there was no practical incentive to adopt a monetary economy. Furthermore, by the fifth century the vast majority of Phoenician trade had moved away from the coinage economies of Greece and was now centred on the Achaemenid empire, which also operated an economy of exchange. With much of Asia Minor still utilising the age-old barter system there was little need for coinage and thus it was not until the influx into the region of Greek businessmen following the Persian Wars that Phoenicia was provided with a strong impetus for change. The earliest Phoenician coinage was struck by Tyre in the middle of the fifth century. During the late fifth or early fourth century Sidon, Arwad and Byblos followed suit and the adoption of coinage by these cities probably indicates a growing weakness in the

Fig. 13. Sidonian silver
coin, 400-384 BC
(courtesy of the British
Museum).

Fig. 14. Tyrian silver
shekel, c. 360-350 BC
(courtesy of the British
Museum).

Fig. 15. Punic silver
double-shekel, c.
237-209 BC (courtesy of
the British Museum).

Persian economy and a resurgence of commercial contact with the Greeks. In addition to being a mechanism for exchange, coinage was also an instrument of political expression with many cities minting coins in order to convey their autonomy or civic prestige. This certainly seems to have been a consideration for the Phoenician city-states who had all suffered defeats at the hands of the Greeks, denting their civic pride. This also explains why three of the main Phoenician commercial centres, Sidon, Byblos and Arwad, chose to depict a war galley, a potent symbol of Phoenician military might, on their coinage. Tyre in comparison chose to depict a flying dolphin and a murex shell, both of which have obvious connections to the city's maritime persuasion.

The mainland Phoenician cities might also have felt pressured to mint coinage due to the adoption of a monetary economy by Kition on Cyprus. Kition first introduced coinage during the reign of king Baalmilk I (479-449 BC) and this must surely have influenced the decision of Tyre, the colony's mother-city, to convert to a monetary economy. The economic role of Phoenician coinage is still unclear; initially, it seems that the coins were circulated as a type of measured bullion, and it is not until the start of the fourth century that coins were produced in large enough quantities that they could be used in commercial exchanges. In Byblos the discovery of small denomination coins made from bronze and silver, which date to the second quarter of the third century, suggests that at least part of Phoenicia was operating a monetary economy. The coinage of the four main commercial centres had vastly different distribution patterns: Tyre and Sidon's were commonly exported beyond the borders of Phoenicia; Arwad's had a fairly limited regional distribution; while the coinage of Byblos seems to have been used exclusively within the city limits. Aside from these four commercial centres, none of the other Phoenician cities can be found minting their own coins until the start of the Hellenistic period. The weight standards on which each of the various cities' coinage was based are poorly documented and thus poorly understood. Arwad, like the cities on Cyprus, seems to have adopted the Persian standard whereas the other cities had their own system based upon shekels of differing weights (from 6 to 13 g per coin). Early issues of Phoenician coinage were minted exclusively in silver shekels, primarily due to the dominance of the Persian daric which was struck in gold. Sidon, as a statement of its superior status amongst the Phoenician city-states, was the only city to issue the double shekel, a coin of considerable value and prestige. The discovery of cast lead weights of triangular and cubic shape, which date to the final years of the first millennium, and which all bear different marks denoting the minting authority (such as symbols or letters), clearly demonstrates that different standards were adopted by each city-state.

Ezekiel and Homer as sources for Phoenician trade
The Homeric texts are important sources of information for Phoenician maritime trade as they provide an insight into early commercial contact between Phoenicia and Greece. The situation depicted in Homer's texts and in the Trojan cycle is one in which Greek society is in contact with Eastern navigators for the first time. The trade Homer describes is not 'organised' in the traditional sense but is in essence individual enterprise operated independently by Phoenician merchants seeking to establish new markets in Greece. In general, early trade was in small luxury items and commerce was undertaken alongside the ferrying of passengers and trafficking of slaves. It was standard practice for the Phoenicians to beach their vessels in a safe cove or on a sheltered beach, then set up a series of small market stalls and sell their wares directly to local consumers. This type of commerce, which is described and derided by Homer, is not that undertaken by aristocrats but that of the professional merchant or *em-*

poros. In the *Odyssey*, Homer records that the Phoenician merchants who visited Greece would spend a whole year sailing from one end of the known world to the other selling their commodities to whomever they encountered. When Eumaeus recounts the story of his kidnap in book 15 of the *Odyssey*, he informs the audience that he was snatched by a group of Phoenician merchants who had established a market on the island of Syrie. These merchants spent an entire year trading with the locals in order to ensure they had merchandise which they could sell or exchange on their journey home. The fact that these men were concerned with a return cargo suggests that they were 'professional' merchants. This idea is supported by Odysseus' lie in book fourteen of the *Odyssey* when he relates the events which have brought him to the court of the Phaeacian king. During the course of his story, Odysseus recounts that while in Egypt he fell in with a devious Phoenician who prevailed upon him to accompany him to Phoenicia where he owned land and a house. Having persuaded Odysseus to join his crew, the Phoenician then attempts to double-cross him and sell him into a life of slavery but the wily hero manages to escape. Interestingly, the Phoenician merchant is recorded as using slave trading to finance his commercial ventures to Egypt, despite being wealthy enough to own his own ship, land and property. This is significant, for whereas trade in Greece was still operating along the principles of aristocratic gift exchange and exchange purely for the purpose of self-sufficiency, the Phoenician merchants who came into contact with the Greeks brought with them a new ideology: trade for profit. For the first time, the Greeks were exposed to an ideology that suggested trade for profit was an acceptable form of acquisition and that commercial activity could be independent from the world of the elite. This erosion of traditional attitudes and morality is perhaps the underlying reason for Homer's contempt for Phoenician traders: 'they are fine sailors, but they are rogues'. Furthermore, Homer recounts a number of episodes in which the Phoenicians are depicted as unscrupulous pirates who rape and plunder their way around the Aegean. However, despite this negativity, Homer's narrative also reveals that Phoenician merchants were regularly welcomed in Greece. Moreover, Homer also displays a deep rooted respect for the craftsmanship of the Phoenicians. For instance, Paris is said to have acquired a piece of Sidonian cloth to give to Helen before carrying her off to Troy; Achilles offers a large silver crater 'a masterpiece of Sidonian craftsmanship' and 'the loveliest thing in the world' as a prize in the funeral games devoted to Patroclus; and, finally, reference is made to another chased silver crater with a rim of gold, which is offered to Menelaus while he is staying as a guest-friend of the king of Sidon. The

Homeric texts suggest that by the sixth century Phoenician merchants were regular visitors to the ports of Lemnos, Pilos, Ithaca, Crete, Syros, Libya, and Egypt.

Phoenician merchant vessels

The first explicit mention of Phoenician ships is a reference to a fleet of 40 merchant vessels carrying cedar to Egypt in *c.* 3000 BC. From the middle of the third millennium there is evidence of large merchant vessels traversing the seas between Egypt and Phoenicia. In general, Phoenician merchant vessels had rounded hulls and, because of this, are what modern sailors would call 'tubs'. To the ancient Greeks they were known as *gauloi*. Aristotle likened the sight of these *gauloi* using their oars to tiny-winged insects struggling to fly. Although they could be propelled by both oars and sails, they were generally dependent on the latter. Because of their carrying capacity the Phoenician *gauloi* were ideal for long voyages on the open sea. Each merchant vessel had a single mast of moderate height to which a solitary sail was attached. The sail was a 'square sail' and only provided propulsion when the wind was directly astern (behind). It was attached directly to the yardarm and therefore both had to be hoisted together. As long as the wind stayed constant the merchant captain could use his sail, but if the vessel became becalmed or the wind was adverse, the sail was dropped and the oars would be employed. With a favourable wind and an average weight cargo the vessel could achieve speeds of up to five knots. Merchant vessels are recorded as having small rowing boats attached to them. These would afford the crew a chance of safety if the ship run aground or was swamped at sea. Moreover, these smaller vessels could be used to land cargo on a shelving shore (i.e. a shoreline where the shallows extend far out into the sea, thus preventing deep or rounded hulled vessels from beaching), a use described by pseudo-Scylax. Scholars have no way of knowing if these boats were hoisted up on to deck until wanted, or if they were towed after the parent vessel, although it is generally agreed that the latter scenario is the most plausible. Despite lacking the substantial storage of merchant vessels built by other contemporary cultures, Phoenician cargo vessels were still famed for their ability to transport large quantities of cargo safely and efficiently. Although scholars do not know the exact carrying capacity of these cargo ships some of the Ugarit texts point toward a limit of 450 tons. Xenophon pays tribute to the meticulous organisation of Phoenician merchant vessels by having Ischomachus suggest that they were so accurately arranged that they could serve as a metaphorical template for the administration and organisation of the ideal state.

Until the middle of the twentieth century, our knowledge of Phoenician naval technology and how it evolved was based on the representation of these ships on frescoes, vases, coins and other ancient artefacts. Since then the discovery of shipwrecks dating from the Bronze and Iron Ages have helped refine this knowledge and improve our understanding. The first Phoenician wreck to be excavated was in 1958 when a local sponge diver told the American journalist Peter Throckmorton about a wreck lying just off the coast of Turkey. In the following year, Throckmorton located the site himself and realised it was the oldest wreck ever discovered, dating to the early Bronze Age. Believing that underwater excavations could be conducted using the same techniques and rigid methodologies as those on land, he assembled a team of scholars from the University of Pennsylvania and set about recovering the wreck. The excavation was a major innovation as it was the first time that archaeologists had attempted to study an underwater site *in situ*, without using professional divers as intermediaries. The wreck turned out to be that of a merchant vessel that had pierced its hull on a submerged outcrop of rock around 1200 BC. The ship had been transporting a cargo of copper and bronze from Cyprus and was Phoenician (strictly speaking Canaanite) in origin. Since Throckmorton, a number of Phoenician ships have been scientifically excavated, including the Marsala wreck, the Ma'agan Mikhael wreck, the Mazarron wreck, the Tanit and Elissa wrecks, and the Melkarth wreck. These excavations have helped historians chart Phoenician trade routes and have yielded material evidence of the nature of the cargoes being transported back and forth across the Mediterranean. Furthermore, all of the vessels which have been recovered have provided a new insight into the construction methods used by Phoenician shipwrights.

The extent to which these wrecks have advanced the scholarly understanding of Phoenician ship construction and sailing techniques is most clearly demonstrated by the Phoenician Ship Project, an ambitious undertaking that seeks to rediscover and document the lives of ancient Phoenician mariners. A group of archaeologists and ancient historians have compiled the findings of archaeological excavations and used them to construct a replica Phoenician merchant vessel (see Fig. 16). Having built the vessel, they tested its capacities by circumnavigating the coast of Africa. In addition to shedding light on methods of construction and the cargoes being transported, shipwrecks also tell a more personal story. In the Tanit and Elissa wrecks it was possible to recover some of the personal items belonging to the crew. Such belongings always provide the best way of determining the location of a ship's derivation or the nationality of its crew, and in these cases they irrefutably confirmed that the vessels were

Fig. 16. The Phoenicia, a reconstructed Phoenician ship (courtesy of Jennie Hill and the Phoenician Ship Project).

of Phoenician origins. The personal items recovered from these wrecks included cooking pots (with close parallels to those found in coastal Lebanon), a handmade bowl, a pestle and mortar used for grinding condiments, a small one-quarter amphora for wine, a wine decanter with mushroom-shaped rim for libations, and a small portable incense stand. Although it was believed that Phoenician sailors drank wine while at sea, the presence of amphorae with resinous linings most commonly associated with wine-carrying confirmed the hypothesis. What was totally unexpected was the discovery of a bundle of cannabis sticks which indicated that the sailors also indulged in a mild form of marijuana tea. The universally accepted suggestion for the purpose of this substance is that it was taken to relax the muscles of the rowers after a tiring day at the oars.

Navigation and cartography
Pliny the Elder assures us that it was the Phoenicians who invented the art of navigation and learnt the rudiments of astronomy which they then applied to navigation. Whether or not this assessment is true, what is certain is that from the Phoenician period until the Middle Ages navigational techniques hardly evolved. In fact modern scholars now believe that Ptolemy, when compiling his famous *Mappa Mundi*, used Phoenician navigation charts as his starting point. Although archaeologists have yet to fully excavate a Phoenician vessel dating to the period of expansion

into the Mediterranean, it is possible to reconstruct Phoenician navigational techniques from historical references and from Assyrian palace reliefs. For a long time scholars insisted that the Phoenicians sailed exclusively during daylight hours in short stretches of between 20 and 30 nautical miles a day. This model excluded night time sailing but did coincide with the fact that the average distance travelled per day fitted with the average spacing of Phoenician and Punic settlements along the North African coastline. Moreover, these so called 'coastal staging posts' were all founded at locations with good natural harbours. However, this theory failed to take into consideration the dangers of coastal tramping (i.e. sailing close to the shoreline). Strong currents, changeable winds and tides, and hidden rocks and sand banks made sailing along a coastline slow and dangerous. Therefore, although coastal tramping is suitable for small-fishing boats and local traffic, it is not appropriate for long distance exchange. Evidence from the eighth and seventh centuries BC suggests that navigation on the open sea and sailing at night were both possible. For instance, Hesiod, when discussing trade, seems to describe trading ventures that lasted for 40-50 days rather than regional or local exchange. Moreover, the *Odyssey* mentions a four-day trip from Crete to Egypt which could only have been achieved by sailing the open seas. Sailing the high seas necessitated travelling at night and therefore presupposes the existence of some system of orientation. Navigating the open sea at night was most easily achieved in ancient societies by the use of the stars as navigational aids, in particular the Pole Star. A sufficiently detailed knowledge of astronomy which would enable navigation at night is clearly recorded in the *Odyssey*; however, it was the Phoenicians who first recognised the importance of the Pole Star. In recognition of this fact, the constellation in which the Pole Star is located, Ursa Minor, was known throughout the classical world as '*Phoinike*'. By recognising that the Phoenicians could traverse the high sea it has been possible to reassess the time it took them to sail from one end of the Mediterranean to the other. New calculations suggest that the crossing from Tyre in the East, to Gades in the south of Spain, a distance of some 4,000 km as the crow flies, would have taken 80 to 90 days. This estimate is based on the average speed of a Phoenician penteconter which was around 10 km per hour. However, given the limited length of ancient sailing seasons it is likely that a ship from Tyre would have to winter in Gades, resulting in voyages to the western Mediterranean taking approximately a year. But what is meant by sailing season? In antiquity, aside from during military campaigns, sailing was restricted to periods of good weather (especially as Phoenician ships were at the mercy of strong tides, currents and winds).

Thus the sailing season for most ancient societies ran from the beginning of spring until the end of October. Herodotus, when describing the first circumnavigation of Africa, records that when autumn arrived the Phoenicians beached their vessels and grew wheat while waiting for the advent of spring and the calming of the sea.

Trade with the interior

Although the focus of much of this chapter has been maritime trade, we should not overlook the importance of overland or river trade networks. The near eastern caravan trade routes, which facilitated the importation of commodities such as gold, ivory, slaves, corn and cattle from Africa, is well illustrated in the biblical accounts. The roads of the ancient Near East were generally unpaved and were essentially levelled tracks which were kept in relatively good condition in order to ensure that trade continued unabated. When the original surface had completely worn away, new roads were created next to the old. In the mountains, building roads meant cutting through obstacles and shoring up paths wherever possible. We know that from as early as the thirteenth century roads were being cut through the mountains using copper picks. This enabled caravans to travel more quickly and easily between Anatolia and Egypt as it prevented them from having to undertake long detours. Travel in the summer usually occurred at night as the heat made long journeys unbearable during daylight hours. Due to the prevalence of bandits and highwaymen, merchants often formed joint caravans. Furthermore, in mountainous and desert regions, merchants often hired local guides or escorts who knew the location of watering holes and river fords. Goods could be carried by wagons drawn by oxen, on light carts drawn by donkeys, or simply by pack donkeys. Given that roads suitable for wagons were rare, caravans of pack donkeys remained the chief method of transport. The animals travelled in single file over difficult terrain; in particularly difficult conditions, even the animals' drivers had to carry some of the goods. If it can be assumed that Phoenician caravans operated in a similar manner to Babylonian, then the length of a daily caravan stage would be 25 to 30 km, while the average carrying capacity of each donkey would be between 65 and 75 kg.

Although lighter goods could be transported overland by pack animals, the coastal sea routes and navigable rivers were utilised when transporting heavier, or indeed bulkier, cargoes. Cargoes that were frequently transported by river-boats include grain, cattle, wood, oil, stone, bricks and people. Assyrian reliefs from the palace of Sargon II depict small riverboats crewed by Phoenicians which are transporting timber. There were two main types of river boat, the coracle and the raft, modern examples of which are still constructed in the same manner as their ancient counterparts. The coracle was a type of round basket, similar to those used by ancient labourers for carrying bricks on their head, and was constructed using plaited rushes that would be covered with skins and caulked. The boat was not particularly deep so, when loaded, the sides only cleared the water by a few inches. The boat was navigated and propelled by two to four rowers. The raft was constructed from the strongest reeds that could be found in marsh land or, preferably, from good quality timber. The buoyancy of the vessel was increased by attaching inflated goat skins below its surface. Once loaded the vessel would be propelled and steered by long poles. These boats were particularly useful in parts of the river which had rapids or shallows. In addition to being used on rivers, both of these vessels could be sailed along the coastline as long as they did not stray too far from the shore.

Chapter 6

Warfare

Warfare was a common occurrence in the ancient Near East and frequently arose from the following causes: a desire to obtain wealth (in particular through the control of commerce or through the levying of tribute), boundary disputes, the need to acquire raw materials (such as timber, stones and metal), or political disagreements. Many Near Eastern cultures, including the Phoenicians, believed warfare could only occur if prompted by the gods and so conflict was often considered a form of divine retribution or punishment. With the geography of Phoenicia encouraging the Phoenicians to become master mariners rather than soldiers, there are few accounts of military campaigns involving the armies of the mainland Phoenician city-states. Consequently, little is known about the organisation of Phoenician armies or the units and personnel deployed during land-based military campaigns. Even the account of the Assyrian king Shalmaneser III's successful military campaign against the king of Arwad in 853 BC provides only sparse evidence for Phoenician military techniques. One of the reasons for this scarcity of information is the political and territorial disunity of the various city states. With a lack of extensive inland holdings and farmsteads the Phoenician cities were unable to equip large permanent armies: instead, when threats arose, they appear to have mustered a citizen levy and supplemented it extensively with mercenaries from Anatolia.

The Phoenician army

The primary weapon of a Phoenician soldier was often one of the tools he used in his everyday life. Therefore, hunters were employed as skirmish troops armed with slings or nets while foot soldiers could be armed with one of a variety of weapons including axes, spears, maces, bows, shields and short swords. From the seventh century BC onwards, iron weapons such as spear points, short swords/daggers, and lances appear regularly in Phoenician graves supporting the hypothesis that the bulk of the army was composed of native levies. The remains of a number of swords, which are in all probability Phoenician in origin, have been unearthed in Sardinia. The blades vary in length from 82 to 130 cm and are commonly

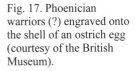

Fig. 17. Phoenician
warriors (?) engraved onto
the shell of an ostrich egg
(courtesy of the British
Museum).

straight, very thick at the centre, but taper off on both sides to form a sharp edge. The point of the blade was blunt and thus the intention cannot have been to use the weapon for both thrusting and slashing, but merely for the latter. Prior to the twelfth century, most spearheads were tanged (sharply pointed), slid into a slot in wooden shaft and then bound in place. Post *c.* 1200 BC the more stable and robust socketed spear became standard issue on the battlefields of the Near East (see Fig. 17). We know that the Phoenicians also used axes and maces as they are mentioned amongst the spoils taken from their Canaanite ancestors by the Egyptians. The archaeological evidence has therefore shown that Phoenician infantry soldiers were well armed in terms of offensive technology but, as a general rule, ill equipped when it came to defence. Consequently, Phoenician troops are rarely depicted wearing helmets, breastplates, or greaves, or carrying shields; moreover, these items are also almost entirely absent from the archaeological record.

Phoenician armies also included large numbers of archers and slingers, both of which could be deployed as skirmish troops. The bow was the principle ballistic weapon of all Ancient Near Eastern cultures. By *c.* 1200 BC the composite bow had begun to see service in Phoenicia and was a weapon which provided considerably more power and accuracy than earlier bows that had been constructed from a single piece of wood. The composite bow was made from different materials laminated together, usually while being held under tension. The Ancient Near Eastern bowstring was generally drawn in the oriental style, i.e. using one or two fingers and the thumb. This allowed a further two or three arrows to be held with the free fingers while the bow was being fired. The Near Eastern bow was designed to be strung using the knee for leverage which increased the tension stored in the string and provided greater range and increased penetrative force. Near Eastern archers are often depicted as shooting from behind a stack of arrows that had been neatly arranged in easy reach; by storing the projectiles in this manner a proficient archer could double his rate of fire. Slings were another prevalent ballistic weapon and had been used in the region since the Neolithic period. Slings were simple to construct, consisting merely of a pouch attached to two long straps and were generally made from leather, papyrus or linen. Although simple to manufacture, the sling was difficult to master and required years of practice to reach full proficiency. During the middle Bronze Age, slingers were casting rocks the size of tennis balls; by the end of the Bronze Age the projectiles had increased in size to that of a cricket-ball. As the favoured weapon of nomadic tribes, the sling is most commonly depicted in Egyptian art as being used by Canaanite mercenaries.

Another weapon, or platform for a weapon, which the Phoenicians are believed to have used, is the chariot. The extensive use of chariots by the Carthaginians prior to the Punic Wars, a technology the settlers brought with them from their mother-city, suggests that chariots would also have been deployed in significant numbers by the Phoenicians of the mainland. Diodorus records that the Carthaginians could field roughly 2,000 chariots; although this is probably an exaggerated figure, it nevertheless highlights the importance of chariots in early Carthaginian warfare. The discovery of large quantities of terracotta model chariots supports Diodorus' claims. The terracotta models are of heavy war chariots that were pulled by four horses and had three crew members. One crewman would steer the horse while the other two were armed with bows and short swords. Although these chariots are categorised as 'heavy chariots' they differed from Assyrian 'battle carts' in having two rather than four wheels. From the limited evidence contained in the annals of the Assyrian kings, it is possible to determine that the Phoenicians occasionally deployed scythed-chariots. The scythed-chariot only had one axle and was usually drawn by a single pair of horses. Sharp blades were mounted on the rear of the chariot and upon the wheel hubs and were designed to cut through the legs of enemy soldiers. The primary purpose of the scythed-chariot was to break through enemy lines and throw infantry units into chaotic disarray.

Fortifications and city defences
Eastern Phoenicia lay at the centre of the overland route between Egypt and the fertile lands of western Asia and was thus a corridor that was in constant use by aggressors marching north to south or vice versa. Conse-

quently, despite being more comfortable fighting at sea, the Phoenicians had to construct cities that were capable of withstanding a siege. City walls were originally built as a way of protecting livestock from wild animals and poachers; some did not entirely encircle the city and seem to have been a preventative measure against flash floods. Once erected, defensive walls became a symbol of wealth and power and could provide a city with political clout. Tyre, for instance, resisted the demands of Alexander the Great because the king believed the city's location (i.e. on an island) and the height and thickness of its walls made it impregnable. Due to ongoing conflicts in Lebanon, the archaeological evidence for the fortification of Phoenician cities remains scant. That the cities of Phoenicia were heavily fortified is, however, attested in a number of Assyrian wall reliefs and in the iconography found on Sidonian coins dating to the early fourth century BC. For example, the Assyrian relief depicting Elulaios' flight from Tyre shows the city as having tall, solid walls that were heavily defended. Tyre is also depicted with high walls on the bronze reliefs of Shalmanesar III that are found on the gates at Balawat, near Nimrud in Northern Iraq (see Fig. 7). Moreover, the strength of Tyre's fortifications is alluded to by the Israelite prophet Ezekiel who mentions obliquely the walls of Tyre when foretelling the city's demise. Indeed, Byblos is also known to have had a series of monumental stone walls that were destroyed and rebuilt on more than one occasion.

Nevertheless, in order to gain a better understanding of Phoenician fortifications during the early Iron Age, it is necessary to examine the defensive architecture found in societies which use comparable construction techniques. The fortifications at Hazor and Megiddo in northern Israel offer useful points of comparison when attempting to reconstruct Phoenician fortifications. At both sites the defensive ramparts comprise thin, towerless parapets constructed from solid brick, while the walls' foundations were composed partly of brick and partly of clay. The number of fortified Phoenician sites increased during the late sixth to fourth centuries BC as the Phoenician cities and towns became defensive outposts for the Persian empire. During this period, the walls at Sidon were expanded southwards while at Byblos the walls protecting the north-eastern flank of the city's acropolis were extended. The Persian period also gave rise to the development of a standardised method for wall construction. This entailed building a number of upright vertical rectangular columns alternating with parallel sections of fieldstone that were in-filled with rubble. As has been seen the 'pier-and-rubble' technique was a method of construction commonly employed in domestic architecture. The defensive walls of Byblos, and almost certainly those of Tyre, Sidon and Arwad, also utilised the more labour-intensive technique of double-faced, dressed ashlar walls that were in-filled with earth and rubble. These ramparts were then strengthened by the application of a gypsum-based cement, a distinctive architectural feature recorded by the Greek historian Arrian. Other developments in defensive architecture made during this period include networks of defensive ditches, the construction of towers and bastions, and the fortification of major port districts.

Naval warfare

The first attempts of the Phoenicians to navigate the Mediterranean were probably as clumsy as those of other ancient cultures. Like most maritime nations the Phoenicians' first seaworthy vessel was the canoe which was roughly hewn from tree trunks. However, the great length of these canoes was quickly found to be unwieldy so they were superseded by the raft. Pliny the Elder records that from an early age the Phoenicians were utilising rudimentary rafts to traverse the coastline of the Levant and Anatolia. The depiction of a Bronze Age Assyrian raft on the reliefs found in Sennacherib's palace provides scholars with an idea of what Phoenician rafts are likely to have looked like. After the raft, the next stage of development was the hulled vessel. Models of this type of vessel have been found in the earliest strata of excavations in a number of Phoenician cities and provide further insights into the type of vessel used during the middle and late Bronze Age. These more advanced vessels had a keel, a rounded hull, high sides, a beak or ram, and a high seat for the steersman. The transition from this type of vessel to the more advanced design, as depicted in the sculptures found in the Palace of the Assyrian king Sargon, occurred quickly and represented a logical progression. The ships depicted on the Sargon reliefs have prows carved into the shape of a horse's head while their sterns are carved into the tail of a fish; each vessel has four rowers who stand to their oars in order to propel the vessel. To ensure stability, both the prow and the stern rise high above the water. The oars are curved like hockey-sticks, and are operated from the gunwale of the ship (i.e. the thick plank that formed a ridge along the sides of a wooden ship). This vessel was still rudderless; however, it did have a mast supported by two ropes that were fastened to both the prow and stern. This mast, which was crowned by a 'crow's nest', had neither sail nor yardarm and therefore does not appear to have been designed with propulsion in mind.

These vessels were to be replaced with the penteconter which, although somewhat larger than its predecessors, was still in the same class (i.e. it was propelled by a single row of oars). Penteconters are a common motif on Phoenician coins and can be identified as having a low bow and an elevated stern. Furthermore, this type of vessel is also well-attested in

Greek art and literature. The number of rowers on a pentecoter varied between 30 and 40 and the vessel, if crewed with experienced rowers, could reach in excess of 9½ knots. Phoenician pentecoters are generally represented without masts and are believed to have been totally reliant on their oarsmen for propulsion. The pentecoter usually had two officers on board and sailed in fleets of up to six galleys. They were organised like genuine naval squadrons and, in general, operated close to the shoreline. Since the pentecoter's carrying capacity was limited, the vessel would be beached at night in order for the crew to collect food and water. Despite its modest size, the pentecoter could still be used to transport passengers, a fact attested by Herodotus in his account of the founding of Cyrene. After a short period, pentecoters were superseded by the more advanced bireme. The first Phoenician bireme can be dated to the reign of the Assyrian king Sennacherib, *c.* 700 BC, and heralded a number of advances in ship construction. The first technical innovation was the introduction of an upper deck; this was an important development as it enabled rowers to be positioned one above the other. This meant that although the bireme was similar in size to the pentecoter it had double the number of rowers. Prototype biremes are clearly represented on the sculptures excavated from the palace of the Assyrian king, Sennacherib (see Fig. 18). In the

Fig. 18. Alabaster wall-panel depicting a Phoenician warship (courtesy of the British Museum).

scene recording king Elulaios' flight from Tyre, two types of vessel are depicted: warships and merchant vessels. Both class of ship have a double tier of rowers, and are guided by two steering oars thrust out from the stern. The merchant vessels are depicted as having hulls which are rounded off in exactly the same way at both the stern and prow and are mast less. In contrast, the warships are longer and thinner, and have a mast and yardarm (to which a sail was closely reefed), situated at their mid-ship. Although the number of rowers on both types of vessel is eight to ten per side, this may simply have arisen from artistic necessity, since a greater number of figures could not be introduced without confusion.

The differences in hull construction and propulsion systems were due to the differing purposes of the vessels. From the sixth century, the main offensive weapon of Phoenician warships was the metal headed ram which was designed to be used in one of two ways; first to be crashed into the hull of an enemy vessel or secondly to shear off an enemy's oar blades when sailing past at close quarters. In times of war, speed and manoeuvrability were of paramount importance so military vessels were designed to be light with shallow hulls. In contrast, trading vessels possessed very deep hulls and were considerably wider; this gave them a greater carrying capacity and ensured they remained stable even in the roughest of weather conditions. Both types of vessel were primarily constructed from the hard resin woods mentioned by Ezekiel in his prophecies against Tyre including cedar, cypress and oak. Soft woods such as pine and fir were reserved for the non-structural sections such as the cabin and the apotropaic eyes carved on either side of the prow. When constructing their vessels, the Phoenicians utilised a method known as the 'shell first' technique. This involved carpenters assembling the keel and hull first, followed by the ribs and deck beams. Once the ship's framework had been assembled they added the outer planking while applying a waterproof coating to the interior and exterior of the hull. The boards and planking were held together with mortise-and-tenon joints that were held firmly in place by long metal nails. Unlike merchant vessels, which due to their minimal crew were cheap to run, the warship was expensive and difficult to equip. At the battle of Salamis (480 BC), it took 34,000 men to crew the 200 triremes of the Athenian contingent. With the combined Phoenician contingent of Xerxes' navy also numbering approximately 200 vessels, it is likely that there were also in excess of 30,000 Phoenician mariners fighting at Salamis.

The superiority of Phoenician war-galleys
The final stage in the development of Phoenician warships was the trireme, a vessel familiar from Greek history. These vessels had three

banks of oars and began to be used by the Phoenicians just prior to the end of the sixth century BC. In antiquity, Phoenician triremes were generally held to be superior to those of any other nation, while Phoenician mariners were considered to be sailors *par excellence*. Although heavier than the bireme the trireme could still achieve a top speed of almost nine knots. The Phoenician trireme differed from its Greek counterpart by having a higher deck, a longer, cone-shaped ram, and a figure head or amulet of protection at its prow. The superiority of Phoenician ships and mariners is clearly attested in Herodotus' account of the mustering of the Persian fleet prior to Xerxes' invasion of Greece. Herodotus records that on the eve of his invasion Xerxes gathered 1207 triremes: this fleet included contingents from Phoenicia, Cyprus, Egypt, Cilicia, Pamphylia, Lycia, Caria, Ionia, Æolis, and the Greek settlements from the Propontis. When the fleet reached the Hellespont, the great king, anxious to test the quality of his ships and sailors, declared that he was going to hold a naval contest. Each contingent that prided itself on its nautical ability selected its finest vessel and crew, and entered it for the great race. Although a large number of vessels took part it was a Sidonian galley that ultimately won the day. Having thus tested the proficiency of the various squadrons under his command, Xerxes rewarded the victorious Sidonians by prom-ising that, from this point on, he would always sail on a Sidonian vessel. The battle of Salamis offers further evidence for the reputation and maritime prowess of Phoenician mariners and vessels. When organising his line of battle Xerxes ensured that he stationed his Phoenician contin-gents on the left wing which put them into direct contact with the Athenians who held a similar reputation amongst the navies of Greece. Despite not carrying the day the Phoenician squadrons are recorded as having acquitted themselves well.

One of the reasons that Phoenician warships (and to a lesser extent merchant vessels) had a reputation for unrivalled quality in antiquity was because they were meticulously maintained. The Phoenicians thought of their vessels as living entities and, because of this belief, ships were considered to be under the protection of the Cabiri. The Cabiri were a group of chthonic deities who were believed to protect sailors and who were often appeased through blood sacrifices; consequently, vessels had to be afforded the utmost care and attention. This belief is also alluded to in the writing of Valerius Maximus who records that the launch of Punic warships were accompanied by a gruesome ceremony in which prisoners of war would be crushed beneath a vessel's hull as it was launched. By smearing the captives' blood directly onto the hull it was hoped that the vessel would be spared from further blood lettings while at sea. Furthermore, all Phoenician vessels were adorned with images of the Cabiri either at their stern or bow. Herodotus suggests they were at the prow of the ship but the Suida and Hesychius place them at the stern. These images were not exactly figure heads as they have sometimes been called but were in fact small and inconspicuous figurines that were regarded as amulets which would preserve the safety of the vessel. There are no representations of these amulets in Phoenician art but it is possible that they may have been no larger than the small bronze or glazed earthenware amulets that commonly protected Egyptian ships and thus too small to depict. Phoenician ships also had apotropaic eyes carved on each side of their prow. The prow was in essence the fulcrum of a ship's navigation and was seen as playing an important part in the success or failure of a voyage. It is therefore unsurprising that these eyes should be so prominently positioned. The *oculus* had a dual origin in the East: first as a counter-charm against the evil-eye and misfortune, and secondly as a visual demonstration of a belief in the ship as a living entity. The *oculi* on Phoenician ships can therefore be interpreted as providing sight to the vessel so that it can 'see' its path and safely chart a route through the dangers of the sea. In addition to the apotropaic eyes, a number of Phoenician and Punic ships also seem to have been adorned with apotropaic horns. These horns, which formed part of a vessel's ornamentation, were intended to further imbue the ship with a zoomorphic identity and protect it against evil.

Chapter 7

Phoenician Religion

The view of Phoenician religion that has been transmitted to us is very incomplete and negative since much of what is documented is found in the records of neighbouring states such as Israel, Babylon and Egypt, or has been written by early Christian authors. Even today some scholars still choose to stress the baseness of Phoenician religion, pointing to its supposed barbaric rites and brutality such as human sacrifice and sacred prostitution, but these are common features that mark many of the religions of antiquity. The only direct sources of information for Phoenician religion are the numerous inscriptions which have been unearthed in the various Phoenician temples. The nature of these inscriptions, as well as their brevity, generally limits the information which can be gained to the names of the primary deities and their general function within the Phoenician pantheon. This evidence can, in part, be supplemented by the archaeological material; however, even when all of this evidence is combined scholars still know considerably less about Phoenician cults and religious practices than those in almost any other contemporary culture. Furthermore, as is unsurprising over such a long history, Phoenician religion underwent marked evolution over time.

The first issue that needs to be addressed is the extent to which Phoenician religious practices drew upon earlier Canaanite traditions. As has already been suggested, the transformation occurring at the end of the second millennium BC divided the region known as Canaan into a series of city-states which modern scholars have designated as Phoenician. This division resulted in a gradual move towards strictly local religious practices. It is, therefore, incorrect to speak of a 'Phoenician pantheon' or more generally of 'Phoenician religion', because each city chose a different pre-eminent deity and had a unique local pantheon. The most important change which occurred relatively quickly after the upheaval of 1200 BC was the abandoning of the Ugaritic-Canaanite gods such as El, Dagan or Anat, and the embracing of previously marginalised deities such as Astart-Astarte. This period also saw the embracing of new deities who had no known direct predecessor; these include gods such as Melqart, Eshmún and Reshef. The study of 'Phoenician religion' therefore presupposes an ideological break with early Canaanite traditions. However, as with so many aspects of Phoenician culture, the pantheon of gods and goddesses and many of the religious practices found within the Phoenician city-states were heavily influenced by foreign cultures. It is therefore possible to identify Egyptian, Babylonian, Assyrian, Greek and Persian influences within the Phoenician belief system. Yet this cultural exchange was not just one way, as Phoenician religion had a considerable impact upon other faiths. Unfortunately, the varying traditions associated with Phoenician deities are on the whole poorly understood and the titles bestowed upon the Phoenician gods and goddesses are often wholly generic, making them distinguishable solely by their regional traits.

Primary deities
The ancient Phoenicians regarded personal well-being as intrinsically linked to the correct worship of different deities. If an individual 'sinned' or a community neglected the proper rites, then evils such as plagues, natural disasters and civil disorder would follow. From the beginning of the first millennium, the number of gods in the Phoenician pantheons was limited, a situation that stands in stark contrast to Canaanite beliefs. There are no triads of deities, as were common in the Canaanite religion; instead, they were replaced with pairs of deities who concentrated and embodied the power and function of the Canaanite pantheon (Tyre = Melqart and Astarte; Sidon = Eshmun and Astarte; Byblos = Baal and Baalat). Each Phoenician city-state can therefore be identified as having its own pantheon comprising unique pairings of gods. This phenomenon clearly illustrates how distinct the Phoenician city-states had become.

In Byblos, the principal male deity was known solely by his title 'Baal' (the Phoenician for 'lord' or 'master'). The term Baal (Ba'al, plural = Baalim or Ba'allm), was a name used throughout the Old Testament to describe the deities of Phoenicia. The term was originally applied to various gods but, by the fourteenth century BC, Baal had become the ruler of the universe. He was worshipped as the source of life and fertility, was seen as the mightiest of heroes, and was often venerated as the lord of war (see Fig. 19). His role as sun god meant that he was also often invoked to protect livestock and crops. Priests therefore instructed the general populace that Baal was responsible for droughts, plagues and other natural disasters. As a result of Phoenicia's trade activities, cults of Baal quickly spread throughout the Mediterranean and Near East. For instance, it is possible to identify the worship of Baal amongst the Moabites and their allies the Midianites during the time of Moses. It is also possible to demonstrate that cults to Baal were widely accepted among the Jews, and,

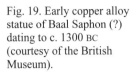

Fig. 19. Early copper alloy
statue of Baal Saphon (?)
dating to c. 1300 BC
(courtesy of the British
Museum).

although suppressed on a number of occasions, never fully eradicated.
Consequently, there were numerous temples to Baal throughout the
Middle East and the name of Baal was often attached to a particular
locality, for example, Baal-Hazor (a village) or Baal-Peor (a sacred
mountain). Most prominently Baal appears in various manifestations as a
storm deity and in these incarnations he is often known as Baal Saphon
or Baal Shamem. As storm deities, Baal Saphon and Baal Shamem posed
threats to maritime trade and transport and both were regularly invoked
as guarantors in bilateral agreements. In a maritime treaty signed between
the city of Tyre and the Assyrian empire, both gods are called upon to
punish potential violators by unleashing violent storms upon their vessels.
Baal's consort, who is referred to simply as Baalat Gubal or 'Mistress of
Byblos', is recorded in a great number of the surviving royal inscriptions
and was seen as being the patron and protectress of the reigning dynasty.
Baalat Gubal is often equated with the Egyptian goddess Hathor and
although her Phoenician identity remains unclear, she appears to have
been distinct from other Phoenician goddesses such as Astarte and Tanit.
Baalat's maternal and fertility functions are clearly attested by her later
association with the Greek goddess Aphrodite.
    The chief deity of Sidon was Eshmun who has been identified as a local

variant of Baal. Eshmun was revered as a god of healing and his sanctuary at Bostan esh-Sheikh is associated with the Yidlal spring, which was believed to have healing qualities. Many of the sanctuaries dedicated to Eshmun are located near rivers, streams or springs, so it seems likely that water was an integral part of the healing ritual. The Greeks associated Eshmun with Asclepius and his popularity is attested by the diffusion of his cult to Tyre and Arwad. Like Melqart in Tyre, Eshmun was also venerated because of his association with death and rebirth. The Sidonians believed that each year Eshmun died only to be reborn; this belief suggests that Eshmun was in some way considered to be linked to the renewal of life through the changing seasons of the year. If this interpretation is correct, it is unsurprising that he should have been paired with Astarte (also spelt Ashtart) who was also linked to fertility and the cycle of life. A close link between these two deities is further indicated by king Eshmunazar's decision to construct their grand sanctuaries adjacent to one another. Astarte was a multi-faceted deity whose functions included dynastic patron, guarantor of fertility, and warrior queen (in essence Astarte represented the philosophy of make love *and* war!). Astarte's warrior nature is clearly highlighted in an agreement signed by the kings of Tyre and Assyria. This seventh century documents calls upon Astarte to snap the bows of either king's army if they renege on the treaty. She was also linked to the mother goddesses of neighbouring cultures and embodied the figures of both heavenly mother and earth mother. Cult statues of Astarte in various forms and guises were buried as votive offerings in shrines and sanctuaries in order to ensure good harvests, fertility, and to provide protection and tranquillity for the home. Astarte was particularly venerated in Tyre where she was linked to the city's primary god Melqart.

Melqart, whose name *Meleq-qart* means 'King of the City', was the deified personification of the ideal Phoenician king. Melqart was frequently regarded as the founder and protector of the city and its colonies. Herodotus, for instance, claims that the worship of Melqart had arisen at the same time as the city and thus it is clear that by the fifth century the deity was already linked to the city's foundation myth. Melqart has no known antecedents in the second millennium and his personality and religious cults are documented only from the time when Tyre was becoming dominant. Like Astarte, Melqart embodied a number of abstract concepts and characteristics and was connected to agriculture, fertility, hunting (Melqart is often depicted as a hunter), maritime activity, civic life and dynastic matters. This flexibility of duties and roles was a characteristic shared by many of Phoenicia's primary deities. Although the agricultural nature of Melqart, a god who dies and is reborn each year in accordance with the natural cycles, was significant, it was, nevertheless, eclipsed by his importance to the maritime life of the city. On the coins from Tyre, Melqart appears as a sea god, mounted on the back of a hippocampus (a mythical creature that had the head of a horse, the body of a winged snake, and the tail of a fish). As god of the sea, Melqart was regarded as patron of shipping. In addition to becoming the primary deity of Tyre, Melqart was also intrinsically linked to the foundation of Carthage. In Carthage, the cult of Melqart had been introduced by Elissa, the mythical foundress of the city, who, it was claimed, brought with her objects sacred to Melqart when she fled Tyre. Furthermore, Elissa's husband had been the chief priest in the temple of Melqart in Tyre: thus both the Tyrians and the Carthaginians saw the foundation of Carthage as being divinely inspired. This belief was so pervasive that the Carthaginians continued to send tribute to the temple of Melqart in Tyre well into the Hellenistic period.

Priests and adjutants

All Phoenician sanctuaries and temples relied on the services of priests, priestesses and other administrators and officials in order to function. Inscriptions found in a variety of Phoenician temples record the roles and functions of these officials. At the head of the religious hierarchy stood the chief priest (or priestess) who was responsible for overseeing the city's cultic affairs. The evidence from Byblos and Sidon indicate that high priests came from families who were closely linked to the royal household. During the Persian period, it was common for the king, or a member of his immediate family (including his mother or wife), to serve as chief priest(ess) and this perhaps reflects a perceived reduction in the power and status of the monarchy. In general, other high ranking members of the priesthood were candidates drawn from the ranks of the traditional aristocracy, with many positions being hereditary. Male members of the Phoenician priesthood are generally depicted barefoot and clean-shaven, wearing a fez-like hat and a long pleated linen tunic which had wide sleeves (see Fig. 20). This image closely matches the description of priests found in the literary sources. According to the Latin author Silius Italicus, the priests of the temple of Melqart in Gades (modern Cadiz) wore white pleated robes, shaved their heads and abstained from sexual acts. Shaving and the ritual cutting of hair were important aspects of the Phoenician priesthood as is recorded in both the epigraphic and archaeological records. An inscription etched on a pottery bowl from Kition records that a man named Moula had shaved his head and offered the cuttings and the

Fig. 20. Detail from the Stele of Ba'aljaton depicting a Phoenician priest (courtesy of Wolfgang Sauber).

bowl as a sacrifice to the goddess Astarte as she had listened to his prayer. In other western colonies, in particular those of Tunisia, Sardinia and Spain, the discovery of large numbers of hatchet razors in both the funerary and temple context highlight the ritual significance of shaving (see Fig. 21). This ritual shaving also accounts for the need for temple barbers.

An inscription found in Astarte's temple in Kition records the key personnel who were employed by the temple. Included on this list are scribes, butchers, bakers, barbers, singers, servants, a 'water-master', and a 'sacrificer'. Cultic personnel took care of the gods' needs, placing offerings, keeping them clothed and sheltered, and performing rituals. However, the majority of the temple staff undertook mundane tasks such as cleaning, guarding property or record keeping. In other Near Eastern temples, cultic staff received regular allocations from the temple's income, namely food, drink, textiles, wool, and occasionally silver; and it is likely that Phoenician temple staff were accorded the same benefits. A number of Phoenician temples are also known to have employed sacred

Fig. 21. Phoenician/Punic ritualistic razor (courtesy of the British Museum).

Fig. 22. Phoenician ivory depicting a priestess (or possibly queen) looking out of a window (courtesy of the British Museum).

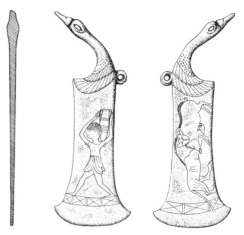

prostitutes. Prostitution was particularly associated with Astarte and her temple on Cyprus is thought to have employed both male and female consorts. Herodotus suggests that some of these prostitutes were ordinary women who temporally gave their bodies as a dedication to the deity in gratitude for an answered prayer or because of a religious obligation. Temples frequently owned large numbers of slaves to undertake menial work or to do hard labour. Orphans, children of the poor and children of insolvent debtors were often dedicated to the temple as slaves, and a large number of these ended up in prostitution. Temple slaves could also be captives of war dedicated by a victorious king, second or third generation slaves born into captivity, or privately owned slaves lent to the temple by a pious master. Most slaves dedicated to the temple were branded in order to prove ownership. Although slaves worked under strict supervision they were normally well-fed and treated.

Cult practices
The various Phoenician cultic calendars, as with those of other Near Eastern societies, were organised according to the agricultural calendar. Sacrifices were offered in celebration of the New Year, the beginning of the ploughing and harvesting seasons, the delivery of the first fruits, and the offering of the first dairy products. Central to this cycle was the spring awakening or resurrection of various earth/fertility deities such as Melqart and Eshmun. A variety of texts also suggest that solar and lunar worship had a significant role in Phoenician religion. The most common festivals were those that were connected with so called 'auspicious' days of the month that could be determined according to the different phases of the moon's cycle. The concepts of regeneration and rebirth were usually associated with the moon as it waxed, waned, and then disappeared once every lunar month. The Phoenicians seem to have believed that the moon died each month and was resurrected by its own efforts to begin the cycle again. Nature clearly formed a particular focus of attention for Phoenician cults and thus many rituals appear to have taken place in the mountains, or in close proximity to water, trees or rocks that were considered to be sacred. A crucial component of many religious rituals or festivals was the cult drama which was re-enacted to institute a necessary function. In the Tyrian festival dedicated to Melqart, which took place in February/March, an effigy of the god was burnt on a ritual pyre only to be resurrected later in the festival. The role played by the average citizen in these events is unclear but at the very least they could observe the proceedings.

As with other cultures, sacrifice was an important aspect of Phoenician worship. Philo of Byblos tells us that sacrifices were commonly performed with animal or vegetable offerings. The office of 'sacrificer' recorded on the Kition inventory presents a tantalising reference of this important but poorly documented part of Phoenician worship. Contemporary parallels from the Old Testament suggest that burnt and blood offerings were common in Phoenicia. The discovery of carbonised bones by archaeologists excavating the Kition temple complex proves that lambs and sheep were regularly sacrificed to Astarte. Although animals were used in the majority of blood sacrifices, there are a number of references which suggest that, in times of extreme danger or hardship, the Phoenicians were not averse to human sacrifice. A more controversial topic is that of child sacrifice. In recent years, two schools of thought have developed: the first group takes the view that the Phoenicians dedicated the bodies of stillborn infants as they were in some way venerated in Phoenician culture, while the second argues that the literary and archaeological evidence points towards the sacrifice of healthy babies. Ancient authors, both Greco-Roman historians like Cleitarchus, Diodorus and Plutarch and church fathers like Tertullian, condemn the Carthaginians for the practice of child sacrifice. Some add lurid but unverifiable details such as the sacrifices being witnessed by distraught mothers, the grimacing victims being consumed by flames, or of human offerings being received by the outstretched arms of a brazen statue. On one point these sources are completely in accord: the Carthaginians sacrificed their children to their supreme deities. If we accept that child sacrifice was an aspect of Carthaginian worship, irrespective of how distasteful it might appear to modern commentators, then it seems highly probable that the original Tyrian settlers brought this custom with them when they settled the North African coastline. In addition to blood sacrifices, the Phoenicians also dedicated more mundane items and archaeologists have recovered thousands of votive offerings. These offerings took a variety of forms including terracotta and stone dedicatory plaques and stelae, utensils, various types of vessels, statues and representations of thrones and miniature shrines. The most common form of votive offering was the bronze or terracotta image of a worshipper or deity. These types of figurines were dedicated in their thousands and the sources tell us that the votive offerings were periodically cleared away into special pits known as *favissae*. The excavation of these *favissae* has provided an unrivalled insight into Phoenician cultic worship. For instance, these offerings have helped to illuminate private domestic cults. In general, it appears that domestic religion tended to focus on issues of primary concern to the family, such as the health and safety of women and children, female fertility, and protection from discord within the home. Female fertility and the protection of infants figured prominently as hundreds of terracotta statues of pregnant women affirm. The discovery of many Egyptian deities represented among the amulets and figurines excavated from Phoenician sites suggests that foreign deities played an important part in private worship. An assortment of inscriptions reveals the extent to which foreign deities permeated Phoenician worship. The popularity of the mother-goddess Isis and the dwarf god Bes documents the growing importance of the Egyptian influence on Phoenician cults associated with healing, fertility and magical protection.

Dance and music, libations, feasting and divination were also important components of Phoenician ritual activity. The centrality of movement in worship and ritual is attested in a number of depictions of votive processions found on metal bowls and ivory sculptures dating to the ninth and eighth centuries. The scenes generally consist of an altar or offering table behind which is seated a goddess (sometimes in effigy form), or a priestess holding a lotus and *phiale* (shallow bowl) or a pomegranate. Behind the throne, musicians play tambourines, pipes and stringed instruments while a procession of priestesses/female adherents bring offerings to the figure seated on the throne. The procession is extended by a chain of female dancers who are holding hands. This type of 'circle' dance was a common feature of other Near Eastern religions, in particular those focusing on goddesses such as Ishtar (Astarte). Dedications and pictorial reliefs indicate that the pouring of libations, including incense, perfume, wine, oil, milk and honey, was common in Phoenician religion. *Phialai* were frequently used in acts of libation. A Phoenician silver bowl from Etruria illustrates a ritual of libation and depicts a procession of priestesses (or water bearers) carrying *phialai* and other vessels which contain the liquids to be used in the ritual. Another central element of Phoenician cults was feasting. Ritual feasting is commonly associated with the *marzeh* ('place of reunion'), which was an elite social grouping that was involved in memorial offerings and sacrifices. Each *marzeh* developed from the sharing of a ritual meal with close friends and kin, in honour of their deified ancestors. In Tyre, these *marzeh* societies became influential in both the political and commercial life of the city, demonstrating that they had more than just a religious function. By the sixth century BC, gatherings of the *marzeh* on festival days were marked by heavy drinking and lavish feasts. Finally, divination was another central feature of Phoenician cultic practices. Diviners (literally examiners) were a specialist group of priests who solicited omens from the gods and then interpreted the signs. Both private individuals and state officials (including the king) consulted diviners on all important matters. Prophecies were often delivered by temple oracles who entered a trance-like state and were believed to become vessels through which the gods would deliver their messages. The Bible records that prophets of Baal would lacerate themselves while dancing feverishly, repeatedly exhorting their deity to commune with them. Omens and portents could also be gleaned through the examination of dreams, animal entrails, and other supernatural phenomena. For instance, the discovery of a series of early inscribed Phoenician arrowheads suggests that belomancy (the study of the flight of arrows) was an important feature of Phoenician cultic practices.

Death and the afterlife
From what Philo tells us, and from our understanding of Ugaritic myths, it is safe to assume that the Phoenicians conceived death as a supernatural being. In Ugaritic mythology death played a prominent role in the early history of the world and was believed to be a chaotic force that threatened the whole of creation. Having lost a conflict fought with the other deities of the Ugaritic pantheon, the power of Death was curtailed so that it had limited dominion over man. Death was not worshipped in any traditional sense, but its power was respected, as attested by the complex nature of Phoenician funerary traditions and rites. While the precise intricacies of Phoenician funerary rituals remain unknown, allusions in the Bible and the carvings on the Ahiram Sarcophagus indicate that death was marked by a period of mourning and ritual lamentation. During this period of lament, mourners would be expected to wear sackcloth, tear their hair, cover themselves in ash and beat their breasts. The discovery of pottery tableware and carbonised food suggests that a ceremonial meal or banquet was enacted over the grave to inaugurate its closure. The fragmentary state of this tableware suggests that it was ritually broken at the time of burial, a practice well documented elsewhere in the Near East. It is also likely that the closing of a tomb would be accompanied by the pouring of libations and/or the burning of incense. Evidence for the latter practice is prevalent in the Phoenician tombs excavated at Trayamar in Spain. The remains, whether cremated or interred, were always accompanied by grave goods such as pottery, jewellery, ornaments, lamps and food. The inclusion of grave goods, in particular food and drink, presupposes at least some concept of material survival as they represent the analogical or symbolic provision of items that will aid the deceased in the afterlife. Furthermore, the remains were frequently adorned with amulets, such as apotropaic eyes, which offer further evidence of a belief in the afterlife and the need for continued protection.

It is impossible to determine precisely what, according to Phoenician eschatology, occurred to an individual after death, but little, if any, distinction seems to have been drawn between the body and the soul. Information gathered from various archaeological excavations suggests that the tomb was considered to be the deceased's eternal dwelling place. For instance, a number of Phoenician inscriptions demonstrate a concern about the violation of the burial site which might disturb the occupant's eternal sleep. Furthermore, the excavation of a number of Punic tombs has revealed that the body of the deceased would be ritually 'prepared' for burial or cremation: this was done by dousing the body with perfumed oil and then wrapping in cloth bandages. For the more affluent sections of society, purificatory rites may well have involved the use of imported aromatics: evidence for this is found on a funerary inscription from Byblos which notes that the deceased was anointed with myrrh and bdellium, neither of which was indigenous to Phoenicia. Having been adorned, the body would then be burnt or placed in the tomb: if interred, the body would either be laid out in a sarcophagus, or, more commonly, simply placed on a rock-cut shelf. In the case of kings, or particularly affluent or important nobles, there are indications that the body would also have been embalmed.

Tombs and cemeteries
The Phoenicians constructed their tombs in a number of different shapes, styles and sizes: however, a broad distinction may be drawn between tombs intended for collective burials and those designed for individuals. The first and simplest variety was the *fossa* grave: these were single occupancy tombs that were in essence a shallow oblong pit excavated directly into soil or soft rock. The second type of burial place was the shaft grave, a narrow vertical well enlarged at the base to accommodate the body. In Carthage, such tombs were frequently far deeper than those in Phoenicia, enabling multiple, laterally cut burial cells. A third type of burial, found at nearly all Phoenician sites and in all periods, consisted of a simple rectangular pit that was of roughly human dimensions: this pit would then be covered by large stones to prevent the body from being disturbed. From the sixth century BC, it is possible to identify a number of variant types of tomb, these range from simple stoned lined pits to elaborate built-stone constructions. If the grave was completely stone lined and covered by stone slabs it is known as a cist tomb: a small number of these sepulchres were also found to contain stone sarcophagi (see Fig. 23). The final type of grave was the underground chamber tomb (*hypogeum*) which could be designed for single or multiple occupancy. The largest known multiple occupancy *hypogeum* was discovered at Achziv

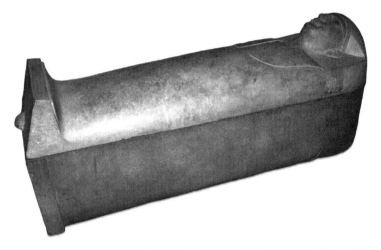

Fig. 23. Sidonian stone sarcophagus, fifth century BC (courtesy of the British Museum).

and contained the remains of 350 individuals. The use of monumental, above-ground tomb structures was a relatively late development in Phoenicia. The most notable mausoleums of this type are the four pyramidal and cube-shaped funerary towers found at Amrit, the earliest of which dates to the fourth century. Throughout Phoenicia's history, infants and miscarried babies were individually interred in large amphorae that would be buried in the ground in order to protect the bodies from scavenging animals.

Phoenician cemeteries were normally isolated from the city by a considerable distance, and, where feasible, by a natural barrier such as a river or lake. This ensured that both spiritual and physical pollution would be kept separate from the city. Island cities such as Arwad, Cadiz and Tyre located their cemeteries on the mainland, again ensuring any pollution was kept away from the city. Most large Phoenician cities seem to have had multiple burial grounds, a situation that arose for two reasons: first because of the settlement expansion which resulted in the need for new burial grounds located further away from the city limits, or secondly because of societal differences (i.e. wealthier citizens wanting to have their own burial precincts). Infant graves are conspicuously absent from adult cemeteries and it appears that children were either buried in exclusive precincts known as *tophets*, or under the floor of the family home. Although the term *tophet* does not appear in any Phoenician texts, it is customarily used to designate an open-air sacrificial area. The term appears several times in the Old Testament, especially in the prophetic books, and is classified as a location where young boys and girls would be sacrificed to the god Baal-Hinnom. Often the accounts of infant sacrifice include crude details that clearly reflect anti-Phoenician or anti-Punic propaganda. Although recording acts of human sacrifice, the biblical sources also indicate that it was an exceptional practice: therefore, it seems that the *tophet* was a sanctuary that performed a public community function, most likely as a location where the remains of infants who had died from sickness or other natural causes, could be interred. As for the ritual killing of human victims, children in particular, this seems to have been a limited phenomenon reserved for particularly dire circumstance. The Phoenicians, then, only resorted to this unsavoury act, which, it must be remembered, was widespread elsewhere throughout the ancient world, when disaster threatened.

Cremations and interment
Archaeology has confirmed that the Phoenicians practised both inhumation (burial) and cremation (burning) when disposing of the deceased. As far as can be determined there was no eschatological difference between the two practices: in fact members of the same family might elect to have different funerary rites. Although cremation was more widely used than burial during the late Bronze to early Iron Age, it appears to have been abandoned for a few centuries before becoming popular again in the Hellenistic period (probably as the result of increased contact with the Greeks). The cremation process took place on a ritual pyre, which was either made within the tomb or just outside the entrance. When the pyre was lit within the grave, the burnt bones were simply left *in situ*, the cranium would then be covered with an amphora or plate, while additional pottery was scattered around the lower extremities of the deceased. The burial site would then be covered by stones. When the pyre was built outside, which was the more common practice, the charred remains of the deceased were collected together and either wrapped in a cloth or deposited in an urn or amphora, which was then placed in the grave. The unguent containers that had been used to prepare the body were now transferred to the grave, while libation vessels were left to mark the location of the burial. If a body was interred in a *fossa* grave, then the burial site would be marked with a crudely carved grave-marker. These markers were shaped from local sandstone or 'beach-rock', and were typically inscribed with a religious symbol and a short inscription. Most inscriptions simply consisted of a personal name, with or without patronymic, and the name of a particular deity, which might include Melqart, Baal, Astrate, El and

Eshmun. Unlike grave-markers excavated at Carthage, which were highly detailed and meticulously carved, Phoenician headstones are crude and irregular, seemingly carved on site by amateur craftsmen unused to working in stone. Nevertheless, the prominent inclusion of ritual symbols, such as the ankh, the sun disk, and the lotus flower, helped to ensure the continued prosperity of the deceased.

Chapter 8

Phoenician Art

What is Phoenician art?

Phoenician craftsmen were lauded in antiquity for their ability to work with metal, ivory, stone and wood, as well as their skill in manufacturing and dyeing fine textiles. Homer for instance states:

> Then the son of Peleus straightway set forth other prizes for fleetness of foot: a mixing bowl of silver, richly wrought; six measures it held, and in beauty it was far the goodliest in all the earth, seeing that *Sidonians, well skilled in deft handiwork, had wrought it cunningly*, and men of the Phoenicians brought it over the murky deep, and landed it in harbour. (*Iliad* 23.740)

Despite having this reputation in antiquity, Phoenician art has often been criticised by modern scholars. These criticisms stem primarily from the fact that Phoenician artists happily borrowed motifs and designs from other cultures. As a result of this 'mimicking', scholars have emphasised the derivative nature of Phoenician art, pointing out that when foreign motifs were copied they were frequently done incorrectly. However, Phoenician art ranges in quality and significance according to the individual artist and the particular function the object was designed to serve. Therefore, when the Phoenicians adopted, and adapted, foreign designs and motifs, they frequently did so for a specific purpose or reason. For instance, Phoenician funerary art was designed with a practical purpose in mind but was also intended to be aesthetically pleasing. So what features, if any, distinguish Phoenician art from that found in other contemporary societies?

In general the primary characteristic of Phoenician art is its eclecticism. It is therefore most easily identified by its adoption of motifs and designs borrowed from other cultures, in particular Egypt, Assyria and Greece. Modern scholars therefore tend to categorise Phoenician art according to the 'borrowed' style which is seen to be dominant. Although scholars still disagree as to which motifs should be assigned to which sub-group, or whether or not it is possible to identify a purely Phoenician style of art, it is broadly possible to divide 'Phoenician art' into the following four categories:

Egyptianising. This term is the one most commonly used to describe Phoenician art. For an artwork to be categorised as 'Egyptianising', Egyptian attributes must dominate the work and the piece must include specific motifs common to Egypt (such as sun disks or images of Pharaoh smiting his foes). Additionally, the piece may incorporate specific elements of Egyptian art such as the regular spacing of figures across a relatively featureless background.

Assyrianising. This term is used to identify Phoenician art which has a strong Assyrian or Hittite influence. Artwork assigned to this category displays motifs such as winged sphinxes (in Egyptian art sphinxes tended to be wingless), Assyrian style lions, Assyrian dress and hairstyles, and Assyrian emblems of royal office.

Cypro-Phoenician. This art is primarily found on Cyprus and is distinguished from the main body of Phoenician art because it draws from Assyrian traditions (see above for the traits of 'Assyrianising' art) rather than emphasising Egyptian iconography.

Syrianising. The similarities in both subject and artistic style mean that it is often difficult to distinguish 'Syrianising' Phoenician art from original Syrian art. However, as a general rule Syrian artists tended to borrow motifs from Anatolia rather than from Egypt. It is also more common for Syrian artists to show figures from a frontal perspective depicting them as shorter and plumper, with distinctive facial features such as large eyes and noses, receding chins and pinched lips. Thus, if a figure is depicted in profile but is adorned in Syrian dress it is likely to be Phoenician artwork.

Minor arts
The vast majority of Phoenician art has been found in a funerary context, most commonly as grave goods or offerings. Grave goods were personal possessions that either had sentimental worth to the deceased or were of high value and buried as either a sign of respect or to indicate the wealth or status of those being interred. Items found deposited as grave goods include jewellery, amulets and scarabs of protection, metal bowls, ivory boxes, cosmetic implements such as combs or mirrors, bronze razors and terracotta masks. The commemorative monument itself sheds light on the

Fig. 24. Shallow copper alloy bowl discovered in the Assyrian
palace at Nimrud. Four pairs of winged falcon-headed sphinxes
confront each other (courtesy of the British Museum).

occupant of the tomb and was often highly decorated. Phoenician art was
also dedicated as votive offerings in temples. However, not all Phoenician
art was solely for the purpose of commemorating the dead or worshipping
the gods. Just as in other ancient cultures, artwork was also produced
simply for its aesthetic value.

Metalworking

As we have seen, the reputation of the Phoenicians as highly skilled
metalworkers was well established by the time of Homer. One of the most
prevalent types of metal artefact is the metal bowl (see Fig. 24). These
bowls have been unearthed in a range of archaeological contexts throughout the Near East and Aegean. They range in date from the ninth to the
seventh century and contain a synthesis of cultural styles and iconography. Although these bowls do not display uniform subject matter or
artistic style, there is an underlying theme in the composition and arrangement of the inscribed scenes. Therefore, although the themes of the scenes
may vary, they all have circular central medallions around which are

placed concentric bands of decoration. The primary themes or motifs of the central medallion include animals, plants, heroic duels, duels between animals, duels between mythical creatures such as sphinxes or griffins, the Egyptian Pharaoh smiting his enemies and military campaigns. The central picture tends to be a panoptic representation of the action whereas the concentric scenes normally depict a narrative in sequential episodes. Clear examples of narrative stories are rare although duelling scenes probably represent episodes from lost epics or myths which have been taken out of their narrative context.

The bowls are usually shallow, approximately 3-5 cm deep and 15-20 cm in diameter. The designs on shallower bowls were engraved or etched on the interior while those on deeper vessels were applied to the exterior. A number of the superior quality bowls were made of silver with gold plating (or gold highlighting) and were inscribed with personal names written in a variety of languages. Although some scholars suggest that these may be the name of the craftsman who manufactured the items, in all probability it is the name of the owner. How these bowls were used seems to have been determined entirely by individual preference. Those found in a votive or funerary context may have been used to pour libations or as part of a religious ritual, or they may simply have been a treasured item dedicated as a sign of respect. Many of the shallower bowls found in private contexts have been pierced, indicating that they may have been suspended for display purposes. The decoration of these bowls should not always be seen as indicative of their purpose as it is likely that the iconography would have little or no meaning for a non-Phoenician audience. That Phoenician craftsmen were manufacturing these vessels for export is attested by their decoration which had a deliberately international flavour. For instance, a high proportion of the bowls excavated in Etruria display Egyptian influences. However, the motifs and hieroglyphs have no meaning and thus were clearly not designed for an Egyptian audience. Instead, as is common with 'ancient' Egyptian papyri sold to modern travellers at all of Egypt's tourist hotspots, the aim was to represent the Egyptian 'style' without a need for accuracy. An Etruscan audience would therefore purchase the item for its aesthetic appeal rather than for the accuracy of the hieroglyphs.

The metalworking tradition symbolised in the east by bronze and silver bowls is represented in the western colonies by the manufacture of bronze razors. The razors are most prevalent in the colonies of North Africa, Sardinia and Spain, and seem to take inspiration from similar implements found in New Kingdom Egypt. As a group, the razors date from the seventh to the second century BC. The razors are 20 cm long and flat with a roughly rectangular body and crescent shaped blade on one short end. The handle protrudes from either the middle of the blade or, more normally, is attached to the short end of the implement opposite to the one that has been sharpened. Frequently, these handles are zoomorphic taking the form of the neck of a large bird such as an ibis or perhaps a swan. Birds and animals are also commonly depicted on the blade itself, as are heroes, gods and goddesses, and plants (such as the palm or lotus). The presence of small holes in the upper body of the blade, or the inclusion of suspension rings near the handle, indicates that the razors were designed to be hung up. As razor blades are not included as grave goods in all Phoenician burials it is possible that they were either luxury items or were a symbolic representation of the deceased's occupation or office (e.g. priest).

In addition to bowls and razors, the Phoenicians also used bronze to cast statues and small figurines. Such objects appear to have been mass produced as votive offerings for both domestic and public shrines. The most common design consists of a seated female or male deity who wears Egyptian style dress, and who is positioned with one of their hands extended, palm out, in a gesture of blessing. Although it is frequently impossible to ascertain the sex of these figurines, when in doubt archaeologists have tended to identify them as female. The general style of these statues is reminiscent of the ivory carvings from Sidon and Berytos which will be discussed below. The best quality examples of these figurines, as with the silver bowls, were inlaid with gold or silver foil. Very few examples of these figurines have been found in Phoenicia proper; instead, the majority have been excavated in those towns or villages with whom the Phoenicians had close commercial relations.

Ivory objects
Ivory-carving has a long tradition in the ancient Near East and Phoenician ivories formed an integral part of a flourishing industry. Phoenician ivories first came to light in Iraq during Henry Layard's excavation of the North West Palace of Ashurnasirpal II at Nimrud in the 1840s. Phoenician ivories have since been found all along the Levantine coast, and in Iraq, Cyprus, Rhodes, Samos, Crete, mainland Greece and Italy. The majority of Phoenician ivories date to the ninth and eighth centuries BC. The main ivory artefacts that have been recovered are panels from furniture such as thrones, chairs, footstools, tables and beds (see Fig. 25). However, there were also a number of smaller items including boxes, handles and cosmetic implements. Originally the Phoenicians obtained ivory from the tusks of elephants indigenous to Northern Syria, however by the eighth century these had been hunted to extinction. Thereafter, Phoenician

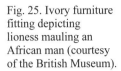

Fig. 25. Ivory furniture
fitting depicting
lioness mauling an
African man (courtesy
of the British Museum).

artisans relied almost exclusively on tusks imported from North Africa with only a small number being imported from India. When constructing furniture, the size of each panel was dictated by the carver's skill at fashioning flat pieces of ivory from curved animal tusks. The more skilled the artisan the larger the panel he could produce. When completed, the ivory furniture panels formed decorative patterns rather than narrative scenes and were attached to wooden frames. If the furniture was of a particularly high quality, the ivory would be decorated with gold leaf, inlaid gems and a colourful glass paste. The individual parts of larger pieces were often marked with Phoenician letters to indicate the correct arrangement and to aid in the assembly of the object, a system which is very similar to that of modern flat pack furniture. The biblical texts indicate that ivory working was an art form specifically aimed at an elite clientele: consequently ivory working was a palace-controlled industry that demanded workers become members of one of the professional guilds. Phoenician ivory workers also seemed to have operated in a variety of workshops outside of Phoenicia proper; for example, the Bible records that Hiram dispatched ivory workers to help in the construction of king Solomon's temple at Jerusalem.

Stone sculpture
Due to the Phoenicians' skill in fashioning portable art they never really developed a coherent tradition in monumental stone statuary. However,

they did produce finely carved relief sculptures that were primarily for funerary or commemorative purposes. These sacrificial monuments – stelae and *cippi* – can be more reliably identified as 'Phoenician' as they occur in uniquely Phoenician cemeteries and are not easily portable. These cemeteries, called *tophets*, were repositories for the cremated re-mains of infants, children and animals. The burials were marked by the erection of a commemorative stone which included an inscribed dedication to the gods. The sacrificial monuments can be up to 1.25 m high and number in the thousands. They take a variety of forms, with the most common being either roughly cubic or, copying the form of Greek tombstone, tall, thin and gabled. The quality of these stones varies greatly. Phoenician masons seem to have reproduced single motifs from a master copy with widely varying outcomes, according to the skill of the individual carver. A number of the stelae seem to have been prefabricated, something suggested by the presence of blank panels on some of the monuments. These panels appear to have been spaces left by the masons for inscriptions that were never added. The discovery of large numbers of stelae has also helped to illuminate Phoenician religious practices as they include a multiplicity of sacred iconography and motifs. To date, nine *tophets* have been excavated in North Africa, Sicily and Sardinia.

In addition to head-stones, the Phoenicians also had a flourishing industry manufacturing stone sarcophagi (see Fig. 23). The earliest known stone coffin is the so-called Ahiram sarcophagus which was excavated in Byblos and dates around 1000 BC. The sarcophagus is rectangular and mounted on squatting lions whose bodies are carved in relief on the long sides, while their heads and tails jut out at each end. Along the top edge of the coffin are carvings designed to represent a garland of flowers. The main reliefs depict two processional scenes: one portrays the king (or perhaps a deity) seated on a throne flanked by winged sphinxes before a table laid out for a feast, while advancing towards the monarch are seven worshippers. The opposite side has four female figures beating their breasts and tearing out their hair; this is thought to represent the period of mourning that followed the king's death. Apart from the Ahiram sarcophagus, all other surviving Phoenician stone coffins date to the fifth and fourth century. The lids of these caskets often took anthropomorphic form, both male and female, with the gender of the occupant being indicated by the headpiece, which was carefully coiffed and sculptured. As expected the earliest examples are heavily influenced by Egyptian culture; however, by the end of the fifth century, they began to become Hellenised and, as they did so, they became progressively flatter and less human in form. To date, more than 100 stone sarcophagi have been excavated from tombs in mainland Phoenicia with Sidon and Arwad yielding the most. This has led scholars to conclude tentatively that these cities were the primary manufacturing centres for stone caskets.

Terracotta
Phoenician terracotta figurines and masks, like the *cippi* discussed above, provide a less diluted insight into 'Phoenician' art as they were designed primarily with the domestic market in mind. The artwork found on terracotta products has been described by Markoe as 'modest, and unpretentious – the product of a "folk" art tradition'. The regional character of Phoenician terracottas can be seen in their general absence abroad while large numbers have been recovered from Sidon, Arwad, Sarepta and, most recently Beirut. Although mainly manufactured for domestic usage, the discovery of a wreck carrying hundreds of clay models of the goddess Tanit suggests that terracotta products were also popular in the Phoenician colonies. Phoenician terracottas can be broadly divided into three main groups: made by hand; thrown on a potter's wheel; reproduced in a mould. In general, the purely handmade objects are more crudely manufactured and roughly finished. Wheel-made items present a more uniform tradition, particularly in relation to figurines, while the moulded items tend to be mass produced and were clearly designed as votive offerings. A common type of figure is the standing nude female with hands cupping or supporting her breasts (see Fig. 26). Another

Fig. 26. Baked clay votive figurine of a nude female wearing an Egyptian style wig (courtesy of the British Museum).

Fig. 27. Phoenician
terracotta mask
(courtesy of the
British Museum).

typical variety is the seated, veiled, pregnant goddess whose right hand is placed upon her abdomen. Both these types of figurine were potent symbols of fertility and were dedicated in order to ensure conception and a safe pregnancy. Other deities were also represented in terracotta, including a bearded male deity wearing a ostrich feathered crown, and a male deity sat on a throne supported by sphinxes. Another popular type of terracotta votive offering was a plaque depicting a miniature shrine resplendent with a pillared colonnade and cult statue.

Another important but less prevalent category of terracotta were masks and protomes (busts): these originate in the late Bronze Age but were popular throughout the first millennium BC. Such types of object have been discovered in both mainland cities such as Tyre, Sidon, Akko and Byblos, and in the western colonies such as Motya and Carthage. The masks are mainly male, but not exclusively so, and have cut-out mouths and eyes (see Fig. 27), the protomes on the other hand are mostly female and are without eye or mouth-holes. As with all Phoenician art they vary greatly in quality according to the individual craftsmen who created them. Both the masks and the protomes are marginally smaller than life size and are either wheel-made or pressed into moulds and then incised or stamped with designs before finally being painted. As with the terracotta figurines, it seems that Phoenician potters worked from a number of master templates; moreover, the discovery of a number of masks with identical defects suggests that they were massed produced.

In 1946, Pierre Cintas divided the masks and protomes found at Carthage into five distinct categories: these classifications are still widely used and are also now applied to items excavated from sites throughout the Phoenician mainland. Cintas categorises the male masks as: (1) handsome, (2) grotesque-old (wrinkled), (3) grotesque-young (unlined), (4) Silenus (a semi-divine figure who has the ears, tail and legs of a horse), and (5) satyr (follower of Dionysus with the ears, legs and tail of a goat).The normal and grotesque masks were also manufactured as amulets which could be worn on necklaces or bracelets. The female masks and protomes are all of the 'normal' variety and fall into roughly one of two categories: those with Egyptian features (such as hairstyle or jewellery) or those with Greek (including veil, oval eyes and/or faint smile). These masks are almost always found in a funerary context and have been variously interpreted as death masks, amulets to ward off evil spirits, smaller replicas of masks worn in religious ceremonies, actual masks used by children or young adolescents in sacred dances, or masks to cover the face of young infants as they are sacrificed. The presence of suspension holes suggest that these masks were designed to be hung and it is possible that they may have been attached to temporary statues to form heads. Unfortunately, as with so much of Phoenician art, the masks offer a hazy glimpse into the world of the Phoenicians, a glimpse which generates more questions than it answers.

Pottery

The distinctive bichrome (two-colour) pottery manufactured by the Phoenicians first appears in the early Iron Age, c. 1050 BC. As a whole Phoenician pottery was designed for the domestic market and its value seems to be derived from its function rather than from its aesthetic merit or quality of manufacture. The early decorative schemes employed a series of broad red or reddish-purple bands which were outlined by narrower black or grey lines. These bands usually encircled the vase horizontally, but, on occasion, could be presented vertically on opposite sides of the vase to form a 'bull's eye' pattern (i.e. filled circles of alternating colours (see Fig. 28). This 'bull's eye' pattern can also be found decorating the interiors of shallow bowls. In general, Phoenician potters were limited in the designs they could inscribe onto their products. The most common decorative patterns consist of combinations of wavy or straight lines, six or eight pointed stars, hatched banding, pendent triangles, or vertical lozenges (diamond shapes). During the mid-ninth century the bichrome style was replaced by a technique which involved applying an overall burnished red or black slip (coating). This style of pottery continued to remain fashionable until the mid-sixth century when

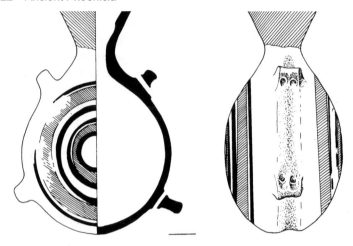

Fig. 28. Phoenician Bichrome pottery pilgrim flask (courtesy of the British Museum).

imported pottery from Greece came into vogue. Phoenician pottery survives in a range of shapes and sizes including bowls, plates, jugs, pitchers, cups, and an assortment of storage vessels. Recent excavations at Sarepta have provided an insight into the methods and processes employed by Phoenician potters. The excavation of a large fieldstone oven coated in baked clay revealed that Phoenician kilns were divided into two levels; the bottom section was used for stocking the flames and for firing the clay, while the top section was used to stack the pottery after the initial firing process. At Sarepta, the firing and preparation were undertaken in different areas of the workshop. Consequently, there were two separate courtyards; in one was the kiln and in the other a potter's wheel and a large circular basin for washing and storing clay.

Faience and glassware
As with their metal working skills, the Phoenicians were also lauded in antiquity for their ability to manufacture glass. According to Pliny, Sidon was renowned for its glass workshops while Strabo reports that the southern Phoenician coastline provided the best quality sand for glass-making. There is literary and archaeological evidence indicating that by the late Bronze Age the Phoenicians were trading in both raw glass and manufactured glass goods: for instance, the Amarna Letters refer to imported shipments of raw glass from Tyre and neighbouring city-states. Although glass working was prevalent throughout Mesopotamia, the Phoenicians are directly associated with the manufacture of thick cast

Fig. 29. A selection of
Phoenician glass
amulets in the shape of a
bearded deity (courtesy
of the British Museum).

glass vessels such as alabastra and hemispherical cups and bowls. These
objects were made using the lost wax method and, once set, were highly
polished in order to make them translucent. Lost wax casting was a
method of producing moulds for metal or glass sculptures. The process
enables the casting of intricate metal or glass shapes by first modelling
the required form in wax and then surrounding it with clay, firing it and
draining the molten wax. This leaves a high quality mould which could
be used for a single casting. Examples of luxury items created using lost
wax casting have been found in Etruria, Spain, Assyria and Crete. Moreover, Phoenician craftsmen also used manufactured coloured glass inlays
for ivory carvings, and a variety of glass charms, amulets and scarabs
which were created using a fine paste (see Fig. 29).

Jewellery

In addition to glass, the Phoenicians also cast jewellery in a number of precious and semi-precious metals. Most of the decorative jewellery that has survived in a good state of preservation was crafted from gold (see Figs 30 and 31). This is primarily due to the fact that silver quickly corrodes in the salty soil of coastal sites while bronze was mainly used in

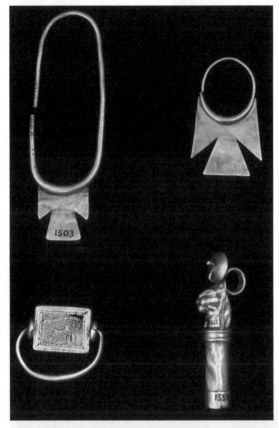

Fig. 30. A selection of Phoenician gold jewellery (courtesy of the British Museum).

Fig. 31. Phoenician gold diadem (courtesy of the British Museum).

the manufacture of more utilitarian items. During the Persian period, Sidon was one of the main centres for the manufacture of high quality jewellery, a fact attested by the discovery of large quantities of exquisite pieces: although a few items have been recovered from a domestic setting the vast majority were found in a funerary context. From these discoveries it appears that for the most part Phoenician jewellery served a magical or protective function. Symbols, such as the Egyptian ankh, eye of Horus, scarab beetle and the winged solar disk are regularly found as amulets or as charms on necklaces or bracelets. An elaborate pendant from Tharros took the form of a bust of Isis-Astarte who is pressing her breasts and wearing a headdress adorned with bull horns, and this item is believed to be a fertility charm. A pendant in the shape of a trireme, discovered at the site of Carthage, is thought to be representative of the type of amulet designed to offer protection to mariners. Aside from amulets, other popular items of Phoenician jewellery included rings, bracelets and ear-rings. Again these items were often engraved or formed in the shape of religious signs or symbols.

Seals

Another item commonly included amongst the grave goods of Phoenician tombs dating to the first millennium was the seal stone or scarab. Although cylinder seals, which were designed to be rolled across wet clay, remained popular in the rest of Mesopotamia, in Phoenicia they were phased out at the start of the first millennium and replaced with the seal stone (or stamp seal). The seal stone was most commonly a gem carved in intaglio which produced a design in relief when pressed into clay. The design on each stone was usually unique thus seal stones operated as a kind of visual signature. Phoenician seal engraving was at its zenith during the fifth and fourth century BC, with production taking place in a number of the western colonies including Carthage and Tharros. As the Phoenician Diaspora expanded, seal stones were crafted from a number of regional stone types including lapis lazuli, amethyst, chalcedony, carnelian, agate, jasper, quartzite, onyx and serpentine. As with other types of Phoenician art, seal stones bear testimony to the willingness of Phoenician craftsmen to adopt liberally Egyptian iconography and merge it with local traditions. It is therefore possible to identify Egyptian mythological creatures being placed within a scene from Phoenician folklore or Phoenician figures carrying Egyptian royal symbols. Later examples bear testimony to an increasing fascination with Egyptian mythology as they take a scaraboid shape (i.e. they were carved in the form of an Egyptian scarab beetle). These became known as scarab seals and were adorned with an assortment

Fig. 32. Phoenician scarab-shaped stamp-seal depicting a god seated on a low backed throne wearing a conical headdress (courtesy of the British Museum).

of Egyptian symbols such as the *ankh*, the eye of Horus, the uraeus serpent, and various symbolically significant birds such as the falcon, ibis and hawk (see Fig. 32). By the early Iron Age, Phoenician seal stones had become standardised in form and so were reduced to depicting a single scene which was framed by a winged sun disk and the Egyptian sign of '*nub*', which signified heaven. The anatomical similarity to a beetle was also reduced with most seals now being rendered as simple ovals.

Textiles

The Phoenicians were renowned for their textile industry: Homer, for instance, records that the women of Sidon were famed for adorning themselves with the most beautiful woven garments, dyed in a multitude of colours, while the biblical prophet Ezekiel, when predicting the demise of Tyre, states that one of the city's chief exports was garments and clothes dyed a deep purple. Brightly coloured garments are also recorded amongst the list of items provided as tribute by the Phoenician city-states to their Assyrian overlords. The Phoenician textile industry seems to have gained its reputation for two reasons: first because the wool, flax and cotton used to create the fabrics were of the highest quality, and secondly because of the intensity of colour that could be achieved from the dye extracted from crushed murex glands (the colours ranged from rose red to a dark violet depending on the strength of the dye being used). Pliny describes how once the glands had been extracted they were heated for ten days in a large vat containing salt water. During this process the dye gradually liquefied and was secreted out of the glands. This liquid would provide colour-fast purple dye when it was re-exposed to the air. Recent archaeological discoveries have begun to confirm Pliny's account. Indeed, excavations at Sidon have unearthed a large dyeing factory which contained two massive heaps of broken and discarded mollusc shells, along with purple stained pottery shards from large storage containers or vats. At the height of demand, this purple dye was worth more per ounce than gold. Tragically, not a shred of Phoenician cloth has been preserved: thus it is impossible to reconstruct the style or appearance of Phoenician made garments.

Suggestions for Further Reading

S. Moscati, *The Phoenicians* (I.B. Tauris, 2001) is the most comprehensive guide to the social, political, and economic history of Phoenicia. It is a compilation of articles by a number of well-established scholars including Sabatino Moscati and Maria Eugenia Aubet. More succinct introductions to the Phoenicians include S. Moscati, *The World of the Phoenicians* (Weidenfeld & Nicolson, 1999) which charts the spread of Phoenician culture throughout the Mediterranean, and provides an overview of the archaeology and history of several important Phoenician colonies; G. Markoe, *The Phoenicians* (The Folio Society, 2006), a richly illustrated book that includes a generous number of photographs of Phoenician artefacts and sites, along with numerous maps and line-drawings; E. Marston, *The Phoenicians* (Benchmark Books, 2002), which provides a comprehensive, although somewhat basic, introduction to the Phoenicians; G. Rawlinson, *The Phoenicians* (I.B. Tauris, 2005), a reprint of Rawlinson's seminal work (first published in 1889) which has greatly influenced modern scholarship on the history and archaeology of the Levant; D. Harden, *The Phoenicians* (Penguin, 1962) and G. Herm, *The Phoenicians: The Purple Empire of the Ancient World* (Gollancz, 1975), both of which, although presenting somewhat dated scholarship, are still nevertheless good primers for those seeking an accessible introduction to the Phoenicians. For a more scholarly but still concise overview of Phoenician history there is also W. Culican, 'Phoenicia and Phoenician colonization' (1991) in J. Boardman et al. (eds) *The Assyrian and Babylonian Empires and other States of the Near East, from the Eighth to the Sixth Centuries BC* (Cambridge University Press, 1991).The most comprehensive resource on Phoenician archaeology is M. Meyers (ed.), *The Oxford Encyclopedia of Archaeology in the Near East,* vols 1-5 (Oxford University Press, 1996). This encyclopaedia details the archaeological and linguistic data pertaining to the broad cultural milieu of the ancient Near East, ranging from prehistoric times up to the early centuries of the rise of Islam, and covering the civilizations of Syria-Palestine, Mesopotamia, Anatolia, Iran, Arabia, Cyprus, Egypt, and the coastal regions of North and East Africa. It includes entries on sites, languages, material culture, archaeological methods, organisations and institutions, and major excavators and scholars of the field. Similarly, R. Weill, *Phoenicia and Western Asia to the Macedonian Conquest* (Ares Publishers, 1980), chronicles Phoenician history from the fourth millennium BC to the Macedonian conquests under Alexander the Great. Weill uses Egyptian and Hittite literary texts to supplement the archaeological record, and, although dated, his descriptions of the sites and objects are still an invaluable resource.

Websites
There is a steadily increasing number of these, but care should be taken to check that the site's owner is a reputable scholar or institution. Both the British Museum (http://www.britishmuseum.org/) and the Louvre in Paris (http://www.louvre.fr/) have extensive collections of Phoenician artefacts and many of these can be viewed online. Another important resource is the Phoenician Encyclopaedia (http://phoenicia.org/) which aims to be the largest web compilation and repository of knowledge about the origins, history, geography, religion, arts, politics and culture of the Phoenicians. The Phoenician Encyclopaedia also maintains a close link with the Phoenician Ship Project (http://www.phoenicia.org.uk/educating-documenting-phoenicia.htm) an ambitious undertaking which aims to re-create the first Phoenician circumnavigation of Africa using a vessel built to Phoenician specifications. Current research on both Phoenicia and Carthage can also be found at http://www.ippsa.net/english/. IPPSA is an international group of scholars committed to the free exchange of research focused on Phoenician and Punic civilization. An array of more generalised information about the ancient world can also be found at http://www.perseus.tufts.edu/hopper/ and http://www.livius.org/.

There follows a small selection of more scholarly books and journals, likely to be found well-stocked public and university libraries, arranged according to the chapters of this book.

1. Defining the Phoenicians
Astour, M. (1965) 'The origin of the terms "Canaan", "Phoenician" and "Purple"', *Journal of Near Eastern Studies* 24, 346-50.
Baramki, D. (1961) *Phoenicia and the Phoenicians* (Khayats, Beirut).
Brown, J. (1995) *Lebanon and Phoenicia: Ancient Texts Illustrating their Physical Geography and Native Industries* (American University of Beirut Press, Beirut).
Röllig, W. (1983) 'On the origins of the Phoenicians', *Berytus* 31, 79-93.
Woodard, R. (ed.) (2008) *The Ancient Languages of Syria-Palestine and Arabia* (Cambridge University Press, Cambridge).

2. A General History of Phoenicia

Bikai, P.M. (1992) 'The Phoenicians', in William A. Ward, Martha Joukowsky, Paul Åström (eds) *The Crisis Years: The 12th Century BC: From Beyond the Danube to the Tigris* (Kendall/Hunt Publishing, Dubuque), 132-41.

3. The Phoenician Diaspora

Aubet, M.E. (1993) *The Phoenicians and the West: Politics, Colonies, and Trade* (Cambridge University Press, Cambridge).

Dunand, M. (1968) *Byblos: Its History, Ruin and Legends* (American University of Beirut Press, Beirut).

Jidejian, N. (1971) *Sidon Through the Ages* (Dar el-Machreq Publishers, Beirut).

Joukowsky, M. (ed.) (1992) *The Heritage of Tyre: Essays on the History, Archaeology and Preservation of Tyre* (Dubuque, Iowa).

Katzenstein, H. (1997) *The History of Tyre: From the Beginning of the Second Millennium BCE until the Fall of the Neo-Babylonian Empire in 539 BCE* (Ben-Gurion University of the Negev Press, Beer Sheva).

Lancel, S. (1997) *Carthage: A History* (Blackwell Publishers, Oxford)

Moscati, S. (1999) *The World of the Phoenicians* (Weidenfeld & Nicolson, London).

Neville, A. (2007) *Mountains of Silver and Rivers of Gold: The Phoenicians in Iberia* (Oxbow Books, Oxford).

Pritchard, J. (1978) *Recovering Sarepta, A Phoenician City*, (Princeton University Press, Princeton).

Negbi, O. (1992) 'Early Phoenician presence in the Mediterranean islands: a reappraisal', *American Journal of Archaeology* 96, 599-615.

4. Government and Society

Avishur, Y. (2000) *Phoenician Inscriptions and the Bible: Select Inscriptions and Studies in Stylistic and Literary Devices Common to the Phoenician Inscriptions and the Bible* (Archaeological Centre Publication, Tel Aviv).

Frost, H. (1973) 'The offshore island harbour at Sidon and other Phoenician sites in the light of new dating evidence', *International Journal of Nautical Archaeology*, 75-94.

Hallote, R.S. (1995) 'Mortuary archaeology and the Middle Bronze Age Southern Levant', *Journal of Mediterranean Archaeology* 8(1), 93-122.

Jigoulov, V. (2010) *The Social History of Achaemenid Phoenicia: Being a Phoenician, Negotiating Empires* (Equinox Publishers, London).

Kempinski, A. (1992) 'Urbanization and town plans in the Middle Bronze II', in A. Kempinski and R. Reich (eds) *The Architecture of Ancient Israel: From the Prehistoric to the Persian Periods* (Israel Exploration Society, Jerusalem), 121-6.

Wright, G.R. (1985) *Ancient Building in South Syria and Palestine*, 2 vols (Brill, Leiden).

Wilson, A. (1945) 'The assembly of a Phoenician city', *Journal of Near Eastern Studies* 4, 245.

5. The Economy

Barnett, R. (1957) 'Early shipping in the Near East', *Antiquity* 32, 220-30.

Betlyon, J. (1980) *The Coinage and Mints of Phoenicia: The Pre-Alexandrine Period* (Scholars Press, California).

Bloch-Smith, E. and Nakhai, B. (1999) 'A landscape comes to life', *Near Eastern Archaeology* 62, no. 2, 62-92.

Culican, W. (1966) *The First Merchant Venturers: The Ancient Levant in History and Commerce* (Thames and Hudson, London).

Oppenheim, A.L. (1967) 'Essay on overland trade in the first millennium BC', *Journal of Cuneiform Studies* 21, 236-54.

Pulak, C. (1998) 'The Uluburun shipwreck: an overview', *International Journal of Nautical Archaeology* 27 (3), 188-224.

Sommer, M. (2010) 'Shaping Mediterranean economy and trade: Phoenician cultural identities in the Iron Age', in S. Hales and T. Hodos (eds) *Material Culture and Social Identities in the Ancient World* (Cambridge University Press, Cambridge), 114-37.

Ward, W. (ed.) (1968) *The Role of the Phoenicians in the Interaction of Mediterranean Civilisations: papers presented to the Archaeological Symposium at the American University of Beirut, March 1967* (American University of Beirut, Beirut).

6. Warfare

Basch, L. (1969) 'Phoenician oared ships', *Mariner's Mirror* 55 no. 2, 139-62; no.3, 227-45.

Casson, L. (1995) *Ships and Seamanship in the Ancient World* (Johns Hopkins University Press, Baltimore).

Diakonoff, I.M. (1992) 'The naval power and trade of Tyre', *Israel Exploration Journal* 42, 168-93.

Elayi, J. (2006) 'The role of the Phoenician kings at the Battle of Salamis (480 BCE)', *Journal of the American Oriental Society*, vol. 126, no. 3, 411-18

Hamblin, W. (2006) *Warfare in the Ancient Near East to 1600 BC: Holy Warriors at the Dawn of History* (Routledge, London).

Lewis, D.M. (1958) 'The Phoenician Fleet in 411', *Historia: Zeitschrift für Alte Geschichte*, vol. 7, no. 4, 392-7.

7. Phoenician Religion

Albright, W.F. (1968) *Yahweh and the Gods of Canaan* (Doubleday, New York).

Aubet, M.E. (2006) 'Burial, symbols and mortuary practices in a Phoenician tomb', in E. Herring et al. (eds) *Across Frontiers: Papers in Honour of David Ridgway and Francesca R. Serra Ridgway,* Specialist Studies on the Mediterranean 6.

Baumgarten, A.I. (1981) *The 'Phoenician History' of Philo of Byblos: A Commentary,* Etudes préliminaires aux religions orientales dans l'empire romain 89 (Brill, Leiden).

Brown, S. (1991) *Late Carthaginian Child Sacrifice and Sacrificial Monuments in their Mediterranean Context*, JSOT and ASOR Monograph Series 3 (Sheffield Academic Press, Sheffield).

Green, A.R.W. (1975) *The Role of Human Sacrifice in the Ancient Near East* (American School of Oriental Research, Missolua, Montana).

Teixidor, J. (1977) *The Pagan God: Popular Religion in the Greco-Roman Near*

Eas, (Princeton University Press, Princeton).

Tubb, N. (2003) 'Phoenician dance', *Near Eastern Archaeology*, vol. 66, no. 3, 122-5.

8. Phoenician Art

Barnett, R.D. (1982) 'Phoenician and Punic arts and handicrafts: some reflections and notes', *Atti del I Congresso internazionale di studi fenici e punici*, 16-26.

Boulanger, R. (1965) *Egyptian and Near Eastern Painting* (Funk and Wagnalls, New York).

Brown, S. (1992) 'Perspectives on Phoenician art', *Biblical Archaeologist*, vol. 55, no. 1, 6-24.

Culican, W. (1970) 'Phoenician oil bottles and tripod bowls', *Berytus* 19, 5-16.

Culican, W. (1975) 'Some Phoenician masks and other terracottas', *Berytus* 24, 47-87.

Culican, W. (1982) 'The repertoire of Phoenician pottery', in H.G. Niemeyer (ed.) *Phönizer im Westen* (Verlag Philipp von Zabern, Mainz am Rhein), 45-82 (plates 4-8).

Gubal, E. (1987) 'Phoenician furniture: a typology based on Iron Age representations with reference to the iconographical context', *Studia Phoenicia 7* (Peeters, Leuven).

Markoe, G. (1990) 'The emergence of Phoenician art', *Bulletin of the American Schools of Oriental Research* 279, 13-26.

Stern, E. (1975) 'Phoenician masks and pendants', *Palestine Exploration Quarterly* 108, 109-18.

Winter, I.J. (1976) 'Phoenician and North Syrian ivory carving in historical context: questions of style and distribution', *Iraq* 38, 1-22.

Index

Roman Egypt
Livia Capponi

ISBN 978 1 85399 726 6

Egypt is by far the best-documented province of the Roman Empire. The dryness of its climate means that an enormous number of literary and documentary papyri have survived – a unique, reliable and lively source that documents Egypt in more detail than any other Roman province. Hitherto these have not been used extensively by Roman historians, on the erroneous assumption that Egypt is somehow 'atypical' as a Roman province. However, scholars now agree that Egypt should be devoted more attention by anyone interested in the history of the Roman Empire.

This book offers a first approach to the subject, presenting a survey of the most important aspects of life in the province under Roman domination, from the conquest by Octavian in 30 BC to the third century AD, as they emerge from the micro-level of the Egyptian papyri and inscriptions, but also from the ancient literary sources, such as Strabo, Diodorus, and Philo, and from the most important archaeological discoveries.

Spectacle in the Roman World
Hazel Dodge

ISBN 978 1 85399 696 2

Gladiatorial combat, animal displays, staged naval battles and spectacular executions were all an important part of Roman culture. The provision of a wide range of purpose-built buildings – from theatres to amphitheatres and circuses – as venues across the empire is testimony to the popularity and significance of these displays.

In this book Hazel Dodge offers an introduction to the main forms of spectacle in the Roman world (human and animal combat, chariot racing, aquatic displays), their nature, context and social importance. She explores the vast array of sources, ranging from literary to archaeological, that inform the subject, examining the spectacles with special emphasis on their physical setting; she also considers the variation in the provision of venues and their context across the Empire. A final section reviews the modern reception of Roman spectacles, especially those involving gladiators.

Roman Frontiers in Britain
David J. Breeze

ISBN 978 1 85399 698 6

Hadrian's Wall and the Antonine Wall defined the far northern limits of the Roman Empire in Britain. Today, the spectacular remains of these great frontier works stand as mute testimony to one of the greatest empires the world has ever seen. This new accessible account, illustrated with 25 detailed photographs, maps and plans, describes the building of the Walls and reconstructs what life was like on the frontier. It places the Walls into their context both in Britain and in Europe, examining the development of Roman frontier installations over four centuries.

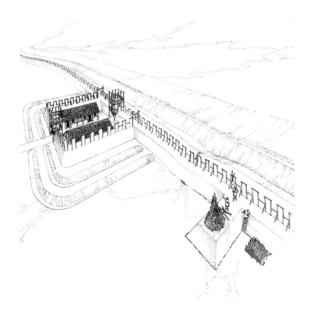

Cities of Roman Italy:
Pompeii, Herculaneum and Ostia
Guy de la Bédoyère

ISBN 978 1 85399 728 0

The ruins of Pompeii, Herculaneum, and Ostia have excited the imagination of scholars and tourists alike since early modern times. The removal of volcanic debris at Pompeii and Herculaneum, and the clearance of centuries of accumulated soil and vegetation from the ancient port city of Rome at Ostia, have provided us with the most important evidence for Roman urban life. Work goes on at all three sites to this day, and they continue to produce new surprises.

Pompeii is the subject of many accessible and useful books, but much less is available in English for the other two cities. This book is designed for students of classics and archaeology A-level or university courses who need a one-stop introduction to all three sites. Its principal focus is status and identity in Roman cities, and how these were expressed through institutions, public buildings and facilities, private houses and funerary monuments, against a backdrop of the history of the cities, their rise, their destruction, preservation and excavation.

Greek Literature in the Roman Empire
Jason König

ISBN 978 1 85388 713 6

In this book Jason König offers for the first time an accessible yet comprehensive account of the multi-faceted Greek literature of the Roman Empire, focusing especially on the first three centuries AD. He covers in turn the Greek novels of this period, the satirical writing of Lucian, rhetoric, philosophy, scientific and miscellanistic writing, geography and history, biography and poetry, providing a vivid introduction to key texts with extensive quotation in translation. He also looks beyond the most commonly studied authors to reveal the full richness of this period's literature. The challenges and pleasures these texts offer to their readers have come to be newly appreciated in the classical scholarship of the last two or three decades. In addition there has been renewed interest in the role played by novelistic and rhetorical writing in the Greek culture of the Roman Empire more broadly, and in the many different ways in which these texts respond to the world around them. This volume offers a broad introduction to those exciting developments.

Early Greek Lawgivers
John David Lewis

ISBN 978 1 85399 697 9

Early Greek Lawgivers examines the men who brought laws to the early Greek city states, as an introduction both to the development of law and to basic issues in early legal practice. The lawgiver was a man of special status, who could resolve disputes without violence and bring a sense of order to his community by proposing comprehensive norms of ethical conduct. He established those norms in the form of oral or written laws. Crete, under king Minos, became an example of the ideal community for later Greeks, such as Plato. The unwritten laws of Lycurgus established the foundations of the Spartan state, in contrast with the written laws of Solon in Athens. Other lawgivers illustrate particular issues in early law; for instance, Zaleucus on the divine source of laws; Philolaus on family law; Phaleas on communism of property; and Hippodamus on civic planning.

Greek Vases: An Introduction
Elizabeth Moignard

ISBN 978 1 85399 691 7

Greek Vases is an introduction to the painted vases which were an ever-present but understated feature of life in the Greek world between the end of the Bronze Age and the rise of Rome, and, in the modern world, an important component of museum collections since the eighteenth century. The book uses specific illustrated examples to explore the archaeological use of vases as chronological indicators, the use of the various shapes, their scenes of myth and everyday life and what these tell us, the way in which we think about their makers, and how they are treated today as museum objects and archaeological evidence.

Key features of the text include a brief accessible introduction to the vases with school and university students in mind, discussion of the different approaches to vases adopted by their very different groups of users, and an approach designed to help viewers understand how to look at these fascinating objects for themselves.

Athletics in the Ancient World
Zahra Newby

ISBN 978 1 85399 688 7

The athletic competitions that took place during festivals such as that at Olympia, or within the confines of city gymnasia, were a key feature of life in ancient Greece. From the commemoration of victorious athletes in poetry or sculpture to the archaeological remains of baths, gymnasia and stadia, surviving evidence offers plentiful testimony to the importance of athletic activity in Greek culture, and its survival well into Roman times.

This book offers an introduction to the many forms that athletics took in the ancient world, and to the sources of evidence by which we can study it. As well as looking at the role of athletics in archaic and classical Greece, it also covers the less-explored periods of the Hellenistic and Roman worlds. Many different aspects of athletics are considered – not only the well-known contests of athletic festivals, but also the place of athletic training within civic education and military training, and its integration into the bathing culture of the Roman world.